D1622484

future
CHURCH

future CHURCH

ministry in a post-seeker age

JIM L. WILSON

BROADMAN
& HOLMAN
PUBLISHERS

NASHVILLE, TENNESSEE

ISBN 0–8054–3134–9

Published by Broadman & Holman Publishers
Nashville, Tennessee

Dewey Decimal Classification: 262.7
Subject Heading: CHURCH

An earlier version was published by Serendipity House (2002).

1 2 3 4 5 6 7 8 9 10 10 09 08 07 06 05 04

I dedicate this book to two pastors.

A few years ago a retired pastor who was a part of the congregation I was serving stopped by the office to pray for me. Though I don't remember everything he said in his prayer, one phrase does stick in my mind. He prayed, "Lord, bless our pastor as he stands on his Father's shoulders to minister to us." Until that day I never really thought about the advantages I have because I grew up in the home of Larry and Barbara Wilson, but since then I've never forgotten them.

So I dedicate this book to the man on whose shoulders I stand, the Reverend Larry Wilson of Hopkinsville, Kentucky. He is more than my father; he is my pastor and my mentor.

I also dedicate this book to the late Reverend Jack Miller. Jack has always been a great encourager to me. A few weeks before he went to be with the Lord, he and his wife Peggy sat in my living room and listened as I read portions from the book I was working on at the time—this book. Discussing *Future Church* was one of the final conversations I had with Jack before he died. Jack was more than a father-in-law to me—he was my friend. I miss him.

Contents

Foreword   ix
Preface   xiii

Introduction: Moving the World   1

1. Get Creative   11
2. Get Spiritual   37
3. Get Radical   67
4. Get Real   97
5. Get Truthful   129
6. Get Multi   159
7. Get Connected   193

Conclusion: The Lighthouse   223
Afterword   235
Acknowledgments   237
Notes   239

Foreword

by Sally Morgenthaler

The new church is here. It came imperceptibly, like a waft of first spring musk at the tired edge of winter: barely distinguishable yet blowing into the subconscious a sense of much-longed-for visitation. Ah, something new, something that we did not create!

Thus the new church arrived—unannounced and unstrategied. How ironic. After two and some decades of trying to manufacture the new church with the wind machines of formula and program, it came anyway, and with it, a deep and humanly resonant reexamination of American Christendom. From theology, anthropology, and ecclesiology to praxis, nothing has escaped deconstruction. We may not be ready, but I can assure you, God is. And the reality is this: the Future Church is already here, in seminal form, but here. And it is this fresh reality—this untamed, messy genesis—that Jim Wilson describes in this volume.

In the past few years, the new church has at least been recognized as existent. Most often it is viewed by established ministries as renegade overflow, an upstart rivulet trying to make a place for itself alongside the wide, placid banks of aging seeker-style ministries—an adolescent phase of "real" church. Dismissed as either generational identity crisis or philosophical fad, what is clear is that the new American church has now grown from a trickle in the mid-nineties to significant runoff at the turn of the millennium. What it will be in five or ten years is uncertain, yet we would do well to take notice. After all, the Grand Canyon was carved by one well-placed, persistent rivulet.

Many of us launched our boats on the Mississippi of church growth in the past two decades. We dutifully set them afloat in the world of big and simple. We followed those who had built massive riverboats, along with the equally massive paddlewheels of programs to propel them. But the landscape shifted beneath our feet. From big and simple, we entered the postmodern topography of small and complex, transforming American culture from homogenous demographies, seeker-believer compartments, easy answers, and fill in the blanks to diverse neighborhoods, ubiquitous spirituality, paradox, and tell-me-your-story. The boats we need now are kayaks, but having spent our ministry years building and operating riverboats, some of us find ourselves not only up a creek without a paddle but without the expertise to use one if it were handed to us.

Into this crisis of change, Jim Wilson offers a journalist's crucial perspective: here's how otherwise ordinary leaders are navigating the unpredictable waterways of change. He provides a "Narratives from the Headwaters" for those of us on the delta.

There are, by now, scores of books on how the new waterways were formed. (Check for the word *postmodern* in the title.) There are even a few books on how to operate kayaks. But here's one about the new navigators themselves: those self-taught kayakers who were upstart enough to say, "Hey, we're not on the Mississippi anymore!"

The Future Church is here. After you read these stories, you just may want to grab a paddle—any paddle—and get wet.

Sally Morgenthaler is the author of *Worship Evangelism* and founder and president of Sacramentis.com.

Preface

When Archimedes discovered the principle of the fulcrum and the limitless possibility of the mechanical lever, he said, "Give me a place to stand, and I'll move the world." That's exactly what I wanted to do—move the world. God gave me a place to stand, the Monterey Peninsula, but I needed to find a lever to impact the world for Christ. Should I transition the church I was serving from its traditional roots into a contemporary church? Or should I leave it as it was? While I sought the answer to those questions, I discovered another lever, a third alternative—the Future Church.

The word *contemporary* means "up-to-date, current" but not in Christian circles. We use the word to denote a church movement that began and takes its characteristics from the 1980s—the Seeker Age. If *contemporary* no longer means "current" and "up-to-date," then another term must emerge to capture that idea. So what term describes a church that is up-to-date and current? Erwin McManus, lead pastor of Mosaic in Los Angeles, California, says his church is "in the future." Ron Martoia, founding pastor of Westwinds in Jackson, Michigan, says, "The future arrived yesterday; if you wait until tomorrow, you are already too late." The future is now!

Young adults, those we once called "the church's future," are attending these churches today; they are the Future Church. It is as relevant to the post-seeker age as the contemporary church was to the seeker era, but its message resonates more with the doctrine of the traditional church. I liked what I was discovering and began taking steps to lead the church I serve into the future. This book is the product of my journey. It shows the seven fulcrum points Future Churches use to leverage culture and move the world and how we are effectively using them in the church I now serve.

Welcome to the journey!

Introduction

Moving
the World

I've only made a few decisions in my life that had the feel of destiny about them. There was the day I stood at the altar in Mayfield, Texas, and told my pastor—my father— that I wanted to accept Christ as my Savior. Then there was a day at a Conference Center in Glorieta, New Mexico, when a missionary asked those who were willing to become missionaries to stand, and I stood. I'll never forget the warm spring afternoon in 1982 when I stood beside Susan Miller on a bridge in the Japanese Gardens in Hayward, California, and asked her if she would be my wife, or the sheer joy I felt, and still feel to this day, that she said yes. It was with that feeling of destiny that I stood before the members of the First Southern Baptist Church of the Monterey Peninsula and accepted their call to become their pastor.

Six months before, when the church made their initial contact with me, I said exactly what I'd told other inquirers, "No thank you, I'm not interested in moving." I wasn't expecting what came next. The voice on the other end of the phone said, "Good, we're not interested in anyone who wants to move." Then she said, "Would you be willing to pray with us that if it is God's will for you to come here he will let us know and he'll let you know too?" What could I say?

This would be a difficult move for me. In all honesty it wasn't that a change in ministry position was totally unappealing to me; it was that I felt guilty for considering a move. The First Baptist Church of Alameda, New Mexico, had stood beside me through my battle with cancer, and I didn't think it was right for me to leave. I owed them too much.

But on the other hand, the idea of going back to California was appealing to me. And this church had potential. After much prayer I came to peace with moving. Yes, I owed a great deal to the people of Alameda, and I always will, but my first allegiance had to be to God, not to a specific church. As I boarded the plane to fly out to speak to the committee, three major obstacles remained.

First, the name—it said something about where the denomination's headquarters are located but nothing about the mission of the church. If I understood this church's ministry, the name was counterproductive to its mission and was hindering it. Second, the governing documents of the church were very restrictive and in my opinion were written to maintain an institution, not to release the people to be the church. Third, because the church was small and located in an expensive area of the country, I wondered if we could afford to live there.

When I hit the ground, I was careful not to let the beauty and raw grandeur of the Monterey Peninsula seduce me. Few places in the world can match its scenery or its climate. Instead, I spent my free time trying to get a feel for the heartbeat of the community, driving through the church's neighborhood and chatting with people in public places.

My interview with the committee alleviated the first two of my concerns and intensified the third. The members of the committee all wanted to change the church's name and felt a new pastor could lead the church to do so. They also felt the church would change its governing documents, or at least seriously consider any suggested changes. (As it turned out, they were right: within the first half year of my tenure, we changed the name of the church to Lighthouse Baptist Church, reflecting the teaching of Matthew 5:16, and changed the bylaws to help facilitate ministry, decentralizing control.)

But I left the interview wondering if we could afford to live on the Peninsula. One search committee member said, "I'm not sure if we can afford to pay you as much as we did our last pastor because we've lost a good portion of our financial base." From what I could tell by looking at the church's finances, she was right. If they paid me what was previously budgeted and Susan went from working part-time to full-time, I knew we could squeak by financially, but now it didn't look as if the church would pay what was budgeted.

When the previous pastor resigned, the church was fairly healthy. It had enough people attending to staff its ministries and pay its obligations. But during the eighteen months the church was without a pastor, most of the military families moved on to their next duty station, and they had not been replaced. It wasn't that they disappeared when the church was without a pastor and would return when they called a new pastor; it was that they were gone. The church atrophied to less than a hundred on Sunday mornings, a couple dozen in the evening service, and a scant handful attending the midweek service. With a heavy debt load contracted from when the church was much larger, the balance sheet had its share of red ink, and high personnel costs could potentially sink the ship.

I chose not to discuss finances with the committee; instead, I left it with, "Give me a call when you decide what you can afford to pay, and we'll make a decision about whether we think we can live on it or not." I know that conventional wisdom is to negotiate before accepting a position because it is the only time a pastor has the upper hand, but I didn't negotiate because the issue for me wasn't money. I knew God would meet our needs if he assigned us to this position. The issue for me was whether members of this church would be willing partners with me in ministry. Would they be willing to "live by faith" and trust in God to meet the church's needs, or would they say in effect, "You live by faith, and we'll live by sight"?

After I left the interview, I called Susan and told her about the wonderful ministry opportunities and how much I liked the people. But then I told her, "I don't think it is going to work out. Perhaps God sent me out here simply to be a consultant for the church." I told her, "During the interview I was able to point out several things the church needed to do to grow, and if they'll do those things, it will have been worth my trip."

During the time that elapsed until my next contact with the church, I prayed, "Lord, if it is your will for me to become their pastor, have the committee offer me more money than was in the budget, not less." *An absolute impossibility,* I thought. I suppose God was testing my motives with that prayer because at the same time a church that was a half-hour's drive from where my parents live asked me to come out in view of a call to be their pastor. The amount they indicated they were willing to pay me matched what First Southern had budgeted, and they would provide a house for us to live in. When you factor in the differences in the Kentucky economy and the California economy and the fact that I could be close to my parents, their new offer was too good to refuse. But that's what I did. I felt it was unethical to deal with two churches at a time, so I thanked them for their interest and promised them my prayers as they looked elsewhere.

Soon after that, I got the phone call. First Southern wanted me to preach in view of a call and would pay me more than was budgeted. Not much more—$200 a year more. But it was more. God answered my prayer. When I accepted their call, I said, "I can't do this job. Not alone. But if we work together, we can change the world from here."

Moving the World

This church is strategically located to influence the world. The Defense Language Institute (DLI) and the Naval Postgraduate School (NPS) are both on the Peninsula. The students at DLI are primarily fresh out of boot camp and are there from six months up to two years to learn a foreign language that they will use as counterintelligence agents and in other areas of service to their country. Most students at NPS are officers working on advanced degrees to enhance their careers. They are all eagles—highly intelligent achievers with uncanny leadership abilities. Rarely do we have them for more than two years, but during that time we have the opportunity to help them become make-a-difference disciples who will be missionaries to the nations where they are stationed in the future. We teach leaders to be servants.

The potential was there, but the people weren't. When we arrived, the church was down to two DLI students and one NPS student. We had two other military families: one was a sergeant assigned to the support staff at DLI, the other worked at Fleet Numerical, a weather forecasting post. All of them had one thing in common: they would go on to their next duty station within a year. Beyond the military institutions the area also has a two-year and a four-year college that the church wasn't impacting at all. There was a lot to do and not much time to do it in. The church was overextended financially, and soon it would lose its only contact with the institutions that provide a golden opportunity to touch the world.

And then there was my inner conflict. I wasn't sure I should try to transition the church from its traditional model to become a contemporary church. I was beginning to question the contemporary church's relevance. I was leaving a church composed predominantly of senior citizens. We toyed with doing a contemporary service there and were taking steps in that direction, but it didn't really work.

Those who attended the contemporary service were coming because of the time, not the style. Some who were attending the service before we introduced contemporary elements to it stopped coming when we began the transition. Within a year we grew the service out of existence; there wasn't enough interest to support continuing it. So we went the opposite direction—we became more traditional. I advertised the church with an ad in the paper that asked, "Are you looking for a church where you can still sing 'Amazing Grace?'" Every time we ran the ad, people came. And the church began turning around.

Before moving to Albuquerque, we had a contemporary service at Berkeley Avenue Baptist Church in Turlock, California, that grew like wildfire and soon overtook the traditional service in attendance. But then again, that was in the early 1990s, and the ultimate result was conflict. Those in the traditional service were willing to tolerate the contemporary one, as long as it was the smaller service. But after the contemporary service grew, the conflict reached a boiling point. This was a major contributor to my departure to Albuquerque.

A contemporary service may have caused conflict in Turlock, but it certainly worked. Why didn't the contemporary model work at Alameda? Was it that the church was older? Or was it because the times were changing? I began to question whether the contemporary church was really contemporary anymore, or whether twenty years had eroded its relevance. *Has the movement institutionalized as it matured and become outdated?* I questioned. As the Amish are time locked in the nineteenth century and the traditional church is time locked in the 1950s, I came to believe that the contemporary church is time locked in the 1980s. One thing I knew for sure: it certainly didn't resonate with the young adults I longed to reach. So what should I do?

The first six months were easy. We had work to do on the governing documents and the church's name; besides, the church needed some time to adjust to me and I to them. But time was running out. Soon we'd lose the few young adults we had. At some point we'd have to make some strategic decisions.

I knew about my church experiences, but what was happening at other churches? I'd just finished covering an Innovative Church Conference for Baptist Press and met some church leaders who were moving away from the seeker model and adapting to a post-seeker approach. I became interested in finding out more, so I secured writing assignments from Christianity Today International, *Growing Churches* magazine, *The California Southern Baptist*, Baptist Press, and *Rev* magazine to explore some of these emerging issues and to interview some of the key leaders of the movement. Assignments fell into place. Later that research would expand and become this book. But in the beginning, I just wanted to find out for myself what God was doing in these times and what changes our church needed to make to reach young adults.

Strategic Planning

My training was telling me to sit down with the church's leaders and write out a purpose statement, a mission statement, objectives, goals, and action plans. But something deep inside my soul was telling me not to. At one deacons' meeting we discussed the issue and decided that we would pray for the Lord's leadership and do whatever he told us to do. That was the extent of our planning. We planned to do whatever God told us to do. And we agreed that when God speaks, he would bring consensus to the body.

Prayerfully we began a faith journey that would transform my ministry and our church—a journey into the future. I worshipped with and interviewed church leaders from across the country who are reaching young adults most churches don't and are effectively transitioning into the future. Some of the leaders were intentional; others were intuitive. Some of the churches were large; others were small. Some were new church plants; others were established churches. Some were traditional churches at one time; others were contemporary. Some were artsy; others weren't.

From these churches I learned seven fulcrum points that helped my church leverage the current culture to reach young adults. I've applied some of the things I've learned from these churches to my church. As you read, don't feel like you need to do all of the things these churches are doing. What you choose to do isn't the point as much as the attitude you choose to do them with. My goal in writing this book is not to give you a recipe to follow; I just want to give you a taste of what other churches are doing. I pray that God will use this book as a catalyst to release your creativity as you leverage culture with these seven fulcrum points to proclaim the gospel in our ever-evolving culture.

In the pages that follow, I explain those seven fulcrum points with three types of sections. Portraits are snapshots of some of the churches I visited that illustrate a fulcrum point at work. Although many of the churches could illustrate several of the fulcrum points, each seemed to exemplify one more than others. The Values section presents some values Future Churches share and shows how they support the fulcrum point at work in the churches. In the Issues sections I examine some changes in our culture and consider how to leverage them for the church's good. In the Conclusion I show what happened to the church I serve as we began using these fulcrum points to move the world.

Please also visit our interactive Web site at www.the futurechurch.com, where you can contribute your own practical ways to implement these fulcrum points in the local church. The site also contains helpful links, interview transcripts, additional information, and pictures of the churches featured in this book.

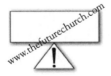

Conventional wisdom says that people don't want to be "preached to" and told how to live. They prefer to set their own rules for living and rely on the entertainment industry—cinemas, sporting events, and theaters—for their inspiration. What is the church's response?

Fulcrum Point 1

Get Creative

I never wore white shoes or slicked back my hair, but I did spend my college summer breaks delivering "hellfire and brimstone" messages in youth revivals throughout the western United States. I was hungry for the chance to preach and appreciated the opportunity to experience different churches. Some of the churches were large, but most were small. They were in metropolitan and rural areas, on busy highways and dirt roads. Even though the churches were different, what stands out in my memory about these churches is their sameness. The worship services were the same in one place as in another. We'd sing a hymn; the pastor would talk a while. We'd sing three more, and the ushers would take up the offering. Someone would sing special music, I'd preach, we'd have an invitation, the pastor would talk a little more, and we'd go home. You could take that schedule to the bank. It was always the same. Every time.

Not anymore. Future Churches are creative. Many of them are welcoming the arts back into the church and are becoming more creative in the way they teach. They model that the Creator God wants his people to be creative. And when they are, he draws them closer to him.

Bumping into the Presence of God
Westwinds Community Church, Jackson, Michigan

Four figures, dressed in black, stand on plexiglas cubes, suspending them above the stage. The upward lighting ema-

nating from the cubes creates an eerie feel as it illuminates the objects the figures are holding: a whip, a hammer and spike, a crown of thorns, and a spear. John Michael Talbot music floods the room as technicians project crucifixion art on the large screen. One at a time, figures dressed in black speak and describe the torture inflicted on Jesus' body by the object they are holding.

"The Roman soldiers used a whip, commonly called the cat-o'-nine-tails, to pulverize Jesus' flesh. The tails of the whip wrapped around his body, and when the soldier snapped the whip, the stones and pottery pieces woven in the leather grabbed his flesh and tore it away, exposing his muscles and sinews to the elements."

As the impact of the first speaker's words sink into the hearts of the worshippers, the second speaker holds up a crown of thorns and says, "When the soldiers thrust the crown of thorns on Jesus' brow, they shredded the flesh on his skull. The thorns on this crown are one to two inches long and extremely sharp. Because the skull is one of the most vascular areas of the body, these thorns would cause severe bleeding when forced onto his head."

Another speaker explains the pain Jesus felt when the Roman soldiers drove nails through his hands and feet. "The spikes were over six inches long and almost a half inch in diameter. The hammer drove the nails through his flesh. Besides the pain from the puncture and slow compression, Jesus felt severe shock waves of pain as the nails touched his median nerve."

The final speaker holds a spear and describes the soldier piercing Jesus' flesh through to his heart. When Pastor Ron Martoia rises to speak, he and the audience explore the question, Why did Jesus do it? Images continue on the big screen and on the small monitors scattered throughout the auditorium. Before communion, the worship team sings "Why?"

The worship leaders don't pass communion out to the crowd; instead, worshippers walk to a sixteen-foot, semi-oval concrete communion table, built especially for this service. Lying on the table are oversized pewter gothic chalices and large loaves. Interspersed with the communion elements are the whip, hammer, crown of thorns, spike, and spear. The silence is interrupted with three loud hammer blows, and the sounds of a thunderstorm. On the screen, these words appear: "You are free to linger as long as you like or go as you like, but please leave in silence." The Good Friday service at Westwinds Community Church in Jackson, Michigan, concludes.

It is graphic and raw. It is also powerful.

At Westwinds the use of art during a worship service is earthy and multilayered. They don't use a painting or a poem to illustrate a point or a drama as an element of a progressive presentation. Instead they weave several layers into a multisensory experience. The music, the art, the lighting effects, the powerful monologues, and visual props form a tapestry that prepares the congregation to meet God at the communion table.

"Worship experiences are 'moment collections' that we design to increase the incidences of bumping into the presence of God," Martoia says. "We hope we are creating moments when people can't help but experience God." At a service a few months before, Westwinds served communion to break a week of fasting. Instead of highlighting Jesus' suffering on the cross, as they did at the Good Friday service, they focused on one of the Beatitudes, "Blessed are those who hunger and thirst for righteousness, for they will be filled" (Matt. 5:6 NIV). That day's "moment collection" incorporated the smell of baking bread, the worshippers' own hunger pains, poetry readings, fast-food commercials playing on television sets throughout the auditorium, art on the big screen, and music. The music included "Breathe," a song with lyrics acknowledging that Jesus is a Christian's daily bread and affirming that believers are desperate for him. These elements didn't give a context for the pastor to preach his sermon; rather, they and the pastor's words created a "moment collection"—a context for Jesus to speak to his people.

The leadership team at Westwinds doesn't target "felt needs of seekers," but neither do they cater to the unique needs of Christ followers. Their ministry addresses "human needs"—yearnings common to all people—needs such as hunger and longing for God. They didn't stumble across this perspective; like most things of value, they gained it the hard way.

Going Deep

When Westwinds opened in January 1987, the vision was to cater to Christ's followers and take them deep into the Word. Martoia was completing a master's degree at Trinity Evangelical Divinity School and planning on going to Scotland for Ph.D. work, when five families from a Bible study group contacted him about starting a church. Martoia was preparing to be a professor, not a pastor, so he was reluctant to accept their invitation. But by June 1986, God did a work in his heart, so he agreed and commuted back and forth to begin planning a church start. "People really wanted a Bible-believing church," Martoia says. "We were going to start a 'deeper in the Word' church." This model fit his gifts, especially since his natural bent was toward the academic. At the time Martoia had an aversion to seeker ministry; he thought the way to grow a church was to "raise up the saints and train them to do evangelism." During the first six years, the church grew to 160, but in that time they had led only five people to Christ. *I could go back to IBM, build bridges to lost people, and lead five people to Christ in six years by myself,* Martoia thought. He came to understand that the church wasn't fulfilling the Great Commission and began to reevaluate their philosophy and methodology.

Seekers and Post-seekers

The church needed to make some changes if it wanted to grow. The board of directors felt that the reason lost people weren't walking through the doors was because of the intensity of the format. "We were doing forty-five minutes of music and forty-five minutes of in-depth Bible study that the average lost person would be clueless about—there is no way they could understand," Martoia says. Lost people have got to be a big part of the mix, the board reasoned; the Great Commission says so. So they asked the question, "How do we create an environment where believers can invite their friends without having to explain what our terminology means?" Martoia's preaching style went through its first major metamorphosis. *I can't keep doing this major, in-depth Bible study, referring to the Greek text, and expect lost people to follow what I'm saying,* he thought.

So the church went contemporary. The service was what Martoia calls "traditional contemporary"—the same kind of service other contemporary churches were doing that included a linear presentation of music, drama, and preaching.

The five years that the church followed the seeker/contemporary liturgy helped the church grow to 380 in attendance, mostly by conversion—a vast improvement. But their best days were still ahead of them.

Something happened as they were changing their format to try to reach the world: the world around them changed. The 1980s were gone, and the 1990s were fading into the twenty-first century. Martoia began to question the seeker model once again, but this time he wasn't on the outside looking in; he was an adherent. It was about this time that Westwinds went through another season of soul-searching because they wanted to find a way to reach the emerging generations. "The contemporary church is calcified in liturgy as much as anyone else is," Martoia says. "The emerging generation is looking at that and saying, 'I can be Catholic, Lutheran, Baptist, or Contemporary.'" To reach the emerging generations, the church had to be fluid and break out of the "calcified contemporary liturgy."

Westwinds' largest growth spurt didn't happen until they adjusted their church to the "post-seeker" era. "Every single worship style has got to be morphed and migrated to the emerging generations," Martoia says. But it wasn't just the need to stay current that sparked their movement into the post-seeker era; it was the understanding that some felt needs universal to everyone prompted the shift. Lost people and Christians have yearnings that worship can satisfy.

"There are three core yearnings," Martoia says. "The yearnings to believe, belong, and become." Today the church doesn't ask, "How do we attract unbelievers?" or "How do we meet the needs of Christ's followers?" Instead we ask, "How do we bring people into a place where God's presence will cause them to yearn for wholeness?"

Because people yearn to believe, the church introduces them to the teachings of the faith. Because they yearn to belong, the church urges them to connect with the "community" of the church. "We don't hold the unanimity value as high as seeker churches do," Martoia says. "If people are walking through the door, they are looking for something, and one of those things is the yearning to belong. We believe the community value is more highly valued than the unanimity value. So we will do all we can to discern, without being intrusive, what they are looking for and do all we can to connect them with it. In our seeker days, we didn't offer much unless they asked for it. Today we bend over backward [to connect with them]."

Those serving at "guest services" work to discern and minister to people's needs and to help them get plugged in to the small-group ministries. Because people yearn to become, they help people answer the question, How can my life work better? That is different from the how-to messages of the seeker church. Preaching on "how to be a better parent" will give the listeners some parenting skills, but it won't fill the deep void inside them. The key isn't applying a "superficial Band-Aid" to their problems; it is to help them connect with God. Hearing a how-to message without encountering God's presence will help people live a better life, but it will not transform them. Only God can transform people's lives. "What we are doing is pointing people toward God and encouraging them to interact with his Spirit," Martoia says. "We say to them, 'Connecting with him is what is going to fill the void in your life and put you on the road to wholeness.'"

Martoia doesn't promise unbelievers that faith will solve all their problems. "We must be careful to under-promise and over-deliver," Martoia says. "We recognize that the human condition is brokenness; while God is in the repair business, repair can be a slow process, and the timing is always in God's hand." Westwinds invites people to plug in to an authentic community where the reality of brokenness and the possibility of healing combine to help people connect with God. "We don't invite people to wallow in their problems," Martoia says, "but to get on the path to wholeness."

One of the ways Westwinds helps people connect with God is through the arts. Certainly God uses the spoken word to speak to his people, but he also uses paintings, dance, sculptures, poetry, or other forms of art to whisper to them, reaching them through its inherent power. Some people aren't "word" people—those who are looking for reasons to believe or principles to follow. They are "image" people—those who long to synchronize their souls with God's will through beauty, rhythm, and intuition. They prefer the picture to the thousand words. The art might create an ambiance for the words, or the words might create a context for the art to impact someone's heart. Which one upstages the other isn't the point. The art doesn't exist for itself, and neither do the words; both elements are signposts pointing to Christ. To put it another way, both are tools God uses to speak to his people. Beauty and truth don't have to be antagonistic toward each other. The one prepares the heart for the other. When done right, words and images partner together to instruct and inspire.

Usually, the different artistic elements melt into a central theme but not always. "Increasingly, because of our multilayering and multitasking, the art may not just be contributing to a theme," Martoia says. "It may provide another way God speaks to people apart from the theme of the day." Art can serve as "off-ramps" from a theme that God can use to personalize a service. It may distract a worshipper from hearing a sermon while enabling her to hear from God. Every week Westwinds's worshippers marinate their souls in a creative environment with a sense of expectancy but not to see something novel or out of the ordinary. It is much more than that. They've come to expect an encounter with the Creator God. And when they come, they can be assured that their leaders have created an environment to increase the incidences of their bumping into God's presence.

And when they bump into his presence, God transforms their lives.

The Arts

On June 25, 1998, the Supreme Court's ruling on *NEA v. Finley* showed the brightest legal minds in America struggling with drawing the line between freedom and responsibility. Four artists whose works often dealt with sexual themes and in some cases involved nude performances sued the federal government because of a law Congress adopted in response to criticism of the funding choices of the National Endowment for the Arts (NEA). One project was a career retrospective exhibit of Robert Mapplethorpe's works, including homoerotic photography, while another exhibit included one of Andres

Serrano's works—a photograph of a crucifix immersed in the artist's urine.

The Supreme Court upheld the controversial 1990 law that required the NEA to consider decency standards when deciding which artists should get grant money. The justices, by an 8–1 vote, overturned a federal appeals court decision striking down the law for violating constitutional free speech and due process protections. "We conclude that [the law] is . . . valid, as it neither inherently interferes with First Amendment rights nor violates constitutional vagueness principles," Justice Sandra Day O'Connor wrote for the majority. The law required that the NEA use "artistic excellence and merit" as the criterion for evaluating applications for funding, taking into consideration "general standards of decency and respect for the diverse beliefs and values of the American public."[1]

In essence, the court's decision said an artist's freedom to create art does not negate the NEA's freedom not to pay them for creating it. Somebody had to make a judgment call. The standard the law stated is "general standards of decency and respect for the diverse beliefs and values of the American public." Good for them! The court struck a blow for decency.

But is this enough? Is it enough to stop funding dark art, or does the church have a responsibility to replace it with the light?

"The twentieth century is unique in human history," says Barbara Nicolosi, Act One, a Hollywood-based summer arts program. "It was the only century in which the arts and faith were separated and antagonistic. Without God's love, art can only speak about one thing with certainty—darkness." Instead of cursing the darkness, Future Churches are shining the light. They are doing two things: they are welcoming the arts back into the church, and they are sending out missionaries into the darkness.

Dramatic Arts

For Easter 2000, the performance arts team of Woodman Valley Chapel in Colorado Springs dressed in period costumes and presented a dramatic musical, *The Choice*, on an elaborate first-century set. This wasn't a drama skit using wannabee actors; it was a full-blown professional presentation, complete with live orchestra music and computer-generated special effects. When *The Choice* ended, the pastor gave a clear gospel invitation, asking the audience to make a choice themselves—a choice to pray to receive Christ as their Savior and Lord.

For some churches the dramatic arts are a high priority. The Church at Brook Hills, in Birmingham, Alabama, designed their auditorium to welcome the dramatic arts. Their stage is as suited for a Broadway musical as it is for a worship service. At the rear is a set of thirty-five different batons (backdrops or scenes). In the foreground is a convertible orchestra pit, and overhead is a computerized lighting system that provides limitless options. With a little work the sound system could be converted to surround sound. On their opening weekend the combined praise teams and band performed the music from their new CD *Whosoever*. With the technical staff introducing theatrical fog and smoke during the performance, it was not a typical worship service.

One Sunday a potter's wheel joined the pulpit and flower arrangements on the stage of the People's Church in Franklin, Tennessee. The service began with the sounds of Darlene Zschech's "Potter's Hand" rushing into the auditorium. A young woman, dressed in costume, strolled to the ancient tool and began to spin the wheel. The camera zoomed in on her hands, so everyone in the two-thousand-seat auditorium could see the clay become a simple vase. On the left side of their projection screen was the dramatization; on the right side, the lyrics of the song appeared. The people worshipped.

The People's Church uses dramatic presentations like the potter's wheel to enhance their worship services. Their congregation loves the multisensory worship experience. After attending the service with the "potter's wheel," Mike, a third-time guest said, "I don't know why, but that was so cool it gave me shivers."

Ambiance Arts

At other churches the dramatic experience begins before the service. Westwinds Community Church in Jackson, Michigan, uses ambiance art to engage worshippers the moment they walk into their auditorium. One week, as worshippers walked into the auditorium, they looked up to see a mannequin with one foot stepping off a suspended ladder into midair. In the sermon Pastor Ron Martoia told the audience, "This is what your life is like without Jesus. Without Jesus, our lives are grounded in midair. . . . We need to get on firmer footing." The visual image stuck in the worshipper's minds, reinforcing the pastor's message. People are still talking about it today.

Then there was the sermon series Pastor Martoia preached entitled "Transformed Hearts." The kaleidoscope team sculpted a six-foot heart and put it in the middle of the stage. Hanging directly above the praise band was a five-foot electrical transformer. The art reinforced the message. It's not about being novel or different to Pastor Martoia. It is about reaching people. "If the mission and the vision [of the church] is to reach lost people," Martoia says, "we've got to do it in cultural languages they can understand."

Fine Arts

Los Angeles's Mosaic speaks several cultural languages. Their name itself, Mosaic, hints at the artistic leanings of the congregation. While Pastor Erwin McManus preaches, artists are working on sculptures and paintings in the audience. McManus doesn't refer to the artists during his sermon; they are not props or visual illustrations. In a way their activity is incongruent with the sermon. They are not there to illustrate or inform; their function is simply to inspire. Witnessing the creative process helps put the audience in the frame of mind to hear the message.

The artists don't distract people from worshipping; they help worshippers connect with God. "We believe everything is connected," McManus says. "When you sit along the ocean and watch waves crash up against the rocks, something resonates inside you for a reason. When you're in the woods, listening to a river, serenity overcomes you for a reason. God created everything to be interconnected as an expression of himself." Experiencing art is one way people connect with God.

Evangelical churches have a long tradition of being "word people." Jacques Barzun, dean of faculties and provost of Columbia College, Columbia University, writes about the Catholic effort to regain ground after the Reformation in his book *From Dawn to Decadence*. "The cultural split in the new life was tangible; the Catholic effort to regain ground produced new works of architecture and the fine arts; the Protestant effort produced literature and large works of doctrine."[2]

Though Evangelicals are more prolific with the pen than the brush, can't our churches welcome artists into our ranks? If we do, perhaps we will see a proliferation of art that magnifies our words. "The ability to express faith and love through dance, through music, through painting is a gift from God," Nicolosi says. "Some people are not word people, so if we say to an artist, 'You have to be a word person like me,' they won't have the means to express what's in their heart, and we shut them down; we make them depressed, isolated, and, in the worst cases, bitter."

Churches that bring the arts back into the church are welcoming artists and art lovers, too. For years, the Chamber Singers of the University Baptist Church in Houston, Texas, have performed classical music as an outreach to the community. "We feel that people will come to this event that won't come to a regular church service," says Matt Marsh, the associate pastor of worship. In November 2000, Pastor Marsh decided to expand the outreach ministry to include an exhibition of fine arts. In an art gallery setting, they set up dozens of areas to exhibit paintings, sculptures, and photography of local artists. Marsh's goal was to allow the artists in his church to use their talents while inviting the unchurched people on their campus "to get them through the door." "I feel very strongly about the arts," Marsh says. "The church is a great home for the arts."

At first glance, art galleries in the hallways and dramatic presentations, modern dance, and sculpting in the auditorium seem a bit strange—out of place. But before the twentieth century the arts were an important part of the church. The use of art as an expression of faith wasn't the exception; it was the rule. Michelangelo's paintings in the Sistine Chapel, da Vinci's *Last Supper*, Botticelli's *Adoration of the Magi*, and Raphael's *Epiphany* are cultural icons with deep ecclesiastical roots. The church was the cultural center. With its art, the church drove the culture; it didn't try to be culturally relevant.

Make no mistake, these twenty-first-century churches aren't trying to be hip or culturally relevant: they are trying to leverage the culture. "Our goal at Mosaic is not to be relevant ultimately," says McManus, "but to cause culture to cause artistic people to say, 'Wait a minute, where is this new way of expressing artistic creativity coming from?'" And when they come to see the art, they encounter God. Whether they are watching a full dramatic performance, participating in a creative worship service, or enjoying a sculpture or painting, something happens when people's creative juices are primed by the arts—their hearts open up to their Creator. As Nicolosi put it, "A beautiful piece of art can stir people inside for something they don't even know. It can make them lonely for heaven."

Missionaries

The Future Church is sending some of its members to become cultural missionaries, to infiltrate the art world with light. Thomas Kinkade, who calls himself a "painter of light," is militant about his desire to spread the gospel through his work. "Art transcends cultural boundaries," Kinkade says. "I want to blanket the world with the gospel through prints. This is a very thoroughgoing form of evangelism."[3]

Bill Myers was a student at the University of Washington, planning a career in dentistry, when he joined some classmates to see the movie *The Godfather*. Because he'd seen only two other movies in his life, *Pollyanna* and *The Parent Trap*, he was outraged by the violence. He staggered out of the theater praying, "God, you've got to get Christian people involved in the motion picture industry."

Within a couple of weeks, he felt he was hearing God's voice, calling him to change his major to filmmaking. Six weeks later, he was in Rome studying film. Today Myers is the cocreator of *McGee and Me*, a screenwriter, and the author of more than fifty books. He also is a cultural missionary, working to bring wholesome entertainment to the world and the light of the gospel to Hollywood.

Twenty years ago Steven Lavaggi's wife left him to marry a writer for *Rolling Stone*. In the process she gave up her ten-year-old son, not knowing that he would be stricken with juvenile diabetes ten days later. As if coping with the personal crisis wasn't enough, Lavaggi also lost his graphic arts business. With his life in disarray, he sat on his bedroom's wooden floor and began searching his Bible for answers. He skipped over the black letters, only wanting to read the words of Jesus. As he read, the risen Christ emerged from the pages. Lavaggi gave his life to Jesus. With time, he felt God calling him to minister through fine art, so he moved to California in order to influence the people who influence the world—Hollywood.

While meditating on Psalm 91:11 ("For he shall give his angels charge over thee, to keep thee in all thy ways"), he began painting a four-foot by five-foot angel. When a friend encouraged him to make the image three-dimensional, he collaborated with a sculptor, and together they cast the angel. Out of his brokenness came a message of hope. While speaking to a crowd of thirty-five hundred people in Soweto, South Africa, Lavaggi held a twenty-inch sculpture of the finished product, a black angel, above his head. When he did, the crowd erupted with enthusiasm. A man on the stage told him that just a few days before, a preacher had said, "One of the things we need is for international artists to express the love of God through art, perhaps even painting angels in black." When Lavaggi heard this, he grabbed a twenty-inch white angel, held it above his head and said, "These angels were created to be like brothers and sisters, even as we are supposed to be." Later, as he reflected on the day, he decided to call the sculptures *The Angels of Reconciliation*.

Lavaggi is a cultural missionary to the world, bringing light where darkness rules. You might say he is an angel of light or perhaps an "angel of reconciliation."

The Story

On January 28, 1986, the Space Shuttle *Challenger* exploded and killed all seven astronauts aboard. It was a major setback in NASA's manned space flight program. Up until the explosion, Americans took profound pride in the accomplishments of our space program. For some there was a thrill in beating

the Russians into space and being more advanced than they were, but there was more to it than Cold War spite.

When I was a child, I would often hear the adults in prayer meetings marvel at the advancements of medical science. If someone had a disease without a cure, Christians would pray that God would aid the scientists as they worked on the problem. These days I hear more about pharmaceutical companies' profits, doctors' mistakes, and insurance corruption than praise for medical science.

Has a bit of our hope died? I can't prove there is a connection between the day our astronauts died and our faith in science eroded, but something has changed. I'd hear people say, "Well, if we can put a man on the moon, then surely we can . . . ." People said that whenever they faced a difficult task or were up against impossible odds. Funny thing, I haven't heard that phrase lately. Did a bit of our optimism die with the astronauts? What was the monumental cause of the shuttle disaster? With the billions of dollars that we put into the shuttle program, it would have to be something big, right?

Not exactly. Seventy-three seconds into the flight, a flame shot out of the side of one of the two solid rocket boosters. The point of failure was an O-ring. Some say it was made from the wrong material, that it was vulnerable to frost. Others say it was too small. Regardless, it failed. And our astronauts died.[4]

Today people reject the notion that rational thought can solve society's ills. I don't know exactly when the shift in thought happened; if I had to pick a date, though, I'd pick January 28, 1986. How can we hope in science when a small thing like a faulty O-ring can kill our heroes? It is as if we've followed the Yellow Brick Road all the way to the Emerald City and looked behind the curtain and learned that the wizard is really just a frail man with no special powers. The brightest among us failed us, and we stopped trusting in them to save us.

Science is not our Savior. The scientific method is not our holy grail. Rationalism cannot save our souls, fix our problems, or give us a better life. If human reason had the answers, wouldn't the experts agree? Would there be any need for second opinions?

If our culture no longer places trust in experts and the scientific method, how should we present the Christian message? Should we say, "I'm the expert. I will tell you the mysteries of life, death, and eternity"? Then should we give logical, rational reasons why non-Christians should forsake their worldview and adopt ours, or should we simply tell our story and let the Holy Spirit convince the hearers? Will the methods of the past work today? Or do we need to make a shift? To answer the questions, let me tell you a story.

An Angel on My Shoulder

Usually I spend more time out in the hallways at conferences than inside, but this one was different. The editor of our denomination's state newspaper couldn't attend the California State Evangelism Conference, so he asked me to cover it for him. I'm not a journalist per se, but I am a writer, so I was happy to take the assignment. He wanted an article that included a quotation from every major speaker. That meant I had to be in every service and that I had to pay attention to every word.

I was typing the keys off my laptop, trying to take down as much as I could, until an "expert" on worship took the microphone. Here's how he began his sermon: "I want to convince you that evangelism should produce worshippers, not just believers." *Convince?* I thought. *Why does he think he has to convince me?* For a brief moment, I couldn't concentrate on what he was saying or the reason I was there. I had a devil sitting on one shoulder shouting at me: "Who does this guy think he is anyway? You're a well-educated, veteran pastor." Then I looked around. *This room is filled with some of the best pastors in California. Who is this guy to fly in from out of state and tell us that he is going to convince us of anything?*

Then an angel whispered in the other ear: "He's our guest, and you shouldn't be thinking like that. Anyway, where's your humility? Besides, he's right. 'Evangelism should produce worshippers, not just believers.'" But the devil wouldn't go away; he chimed in, "If you already believe what he is saying and if all he wants to do is convince you, you really don't have to listen. Tune him out!"

Why did I react to this man's teaching like this? During modernity, teachers proved their points with logical, well-crafted arguments. The assumption was that people would believe what they understood. Experts arose who could give "evidence that demanded a verdict" and call seekers to faith in Christ.

That approach brought many people to Christ. Lee Strobel shares his pilgrimage to Christ in his book *God's Outrageous Claims*. He writes: "I used to consider the Resurrection to be a laughable fairy tale. After all, Yale Law School had trained me to be coldly rational, and my years of sniffing for news at the *Chicago Tribune* had only toughened my naturally cynical personality. But intrigued by changes in my wife after she became a Christian, I spent nearly two years systematically using my journalistic and legal experience to study the evidence for the Resurrection and the credibility of Jesus' claims to being God. I emerged totally convinced and gave my life to Christ."

Strobel didn't come to faith in Christ until he investigated all the evidence and concluded that Jesus was worthy of his trust. Propositional truth convinced him. But it was his wife's story—her conversion experience—that piqued his interest in the gospel. It isn't that the gospel can't stand the scrutiny of investigation—it can. But detail-drenched, propositional teaching isn't the only way to communicate the gospel. It can also be communicated, as Jesus did, in story. Just as there is propositional truth, there is also narrative truth—truth clearly exposed by the story. Jesus said, "Therefore speak I to them in parables: because they seeing, see not; and hearing, they hear not, neither do they understand" (Matt. 13:13 KJV).

Deflated Balloons

Truth is truth, regardless of how it is communicated. The form of communication does not change the content of the truth, but it may change how it is received.

Personally, I'm an e-mail guy. I typically check for e-mail several times an hour. When I travel, I take my computer with me and check it several times a day. If I leave the laptop at home, I can still check my e-mail with my wireless PDA. E-mail is my preferred mode of communication.

A few years ago I got rid of my cell phone. Remember when cell phones had to be installed in cars? I bought one way back then, when they first came out. The installers secured a large box under the front seat and mounted the phone on the console between the seats of my pickup and an antenna on the back windshield. It was a monstrosity.

As the phones got smaller and more compact, I upgraded several times. Then a few years ago I decided to get rid of it. Why? I don't like talking on the phone. Never have. For some reason I'm anxious to get off the phone the moment I pick it up. The truth is, I'm happy to be away from the phone when I'm out of the office, and I can always get to a pay phone if someone pages me. I didn't get a cell phone again until a year later, when Handspring came out with a PDA that also was a cell phone. My big motivation in buying it was to be able to get my e-mail while I was on the road, away from a phone line. People who know me well know that e-mail is the best way to communicate with me.

Just as I have a preferred mode of communication, our culture does too. They'd rather have their truth given to them in story, not in propositions.

Sally Morgenthaller, author of *Worship Evangelism*, says, "We left the oral culture with Gutenberg's press in 1452, but we've rediscovered it through film, television, and the Internet. I think everyone gets e-mail messages forwarded to them, and they are mainly stories. We are now sitting around the campfire of the Internet sharing our stories." Take a minute and go through your e-mail in-box. How many cold, rational facts have people forwarded to you lately? Did you take time to read them? How many touching chicken-soup-for-the-soul-type stories are in there?

The story is powerful. Tell the story. How many times have you been teaching something and said, "It's like the story of the prodigal son where the elder brother got mad," summarizing a powerful story in one sentence? It's like letting the air out of a balloon: it is smaller and easier to carry around, but a bouquet of deflated balloons doesn't cheer up anyone. It just doesn't have the impact. Instead of rushing through the story and referring to it to buttress a propositional truth, why not tell the story and let the truth emerge? God works in quiet moments while someone mulls over a story. The Spirit of God teaches the listeners. They learn by experiencing the story.

Last Easter I didn't talk about the evidences for the resurrection, as I had for twenty years. Instead, I simply told the story of Jesus' death and resurrection. The story has power; I didn't feel the need to prove it, just to proclaim it. It was one of the best Easter sermons I've ever preached.

The story is powerful, and it communicates at the deepest parts of a person's soul. "Postmodern man is as open to the gospel as he has ever been," says Dieter Zander, a church planter in San Francisco. "You don't even have to prove God. All you have to do is tell his story. It's like the strings of a guitar. When you put your face next to an A string and begin to hum an A, that string begins to vibrate. The D won't. The G won't, but the A will. When we hear God's story, something inside our heart starts to vibrate, whether we are Christians or not, because our hearts were created to vibrate with that story."

Teachers don't have to convince people. Because people are created to worship God, they will respond to his story, and they will believe if we will tell his story. The most thrilling thing about teaching is helping people see the God who is standing right behind them and walking with them. And when we tell God's story, something inside them begins to vibrate. They ask, "Could it be true? Could it really be true?" In that moment God's Spirit convinces them, and they believe.

Conventional wisdom says that one religion is as good as another. Christians are often viewed as mean-spirited, narrow-minded bigots. Gurus, mystics, and psychics are as legitimate as priests, rabbis, and ministers in today's supercharged spiritual environment. What is the church's response?

Fulcrum Point 2

Get Spiritual

Matthew 18:20 says, "For where two or three have gathered together in My name, there I am in their midst" (NASB). It is possible to have hundreds of people gather for church and still not have two or three gathered in his name. Without God's presence, a creative church can, at best, only be entertaining. There is nothing wrong with Christian entertainment, but it is a poor substitute for worship.

In his book *The Emerging Church: Vintage Christianity for New Generations*, Pastor Dan Kimball of Vintage Faith Church in Santa Cruz, California, cites a journalist who was writing about a Christian concert he attended. The headlines said, "Christapalooza: 20,000 Christians convene . . . God doesn't show." The journalist wrote: "I have a difficult time locating any similarities between what Jesus says and does, and what the people—in particular the organizers [at this festival] said and did . . . . Jesus is a beacon of righteousness who leads the way through a dark world to eternal peace, love, and eternal salvation; the Jesus of [the festival] is a blue-light special, pointing you to the quick fix of a righteous bargain in the shopping mall of endless consumption."[1]

This journalist Kimball cites isn't alone. The church continues to slip in popularity in our culture. The number of Americans who claim no religious preference rose from around 7 percent at the beginning of the 1990s to around 14 percent at the end of the decade. In an article published in the *American Sociological Review*, University of California at Berkeley sociologists Michael Hout and Claude Fischer explain why the change does not necessarily reflect a decrease in faith: "One of the points we're trying to make is that most people who have no church still are likely to say things like, 'God is real. Heaven and hell are real.'" Popular dissatisfaction isn't with faith or with God, but with the church. Only 10 percent of those with no religious preference expressed a "great deal" of confidence in church leaders and churches. Perhaps that is to be expected. But less than half of people with a religious preference have a "great deal" of confidence in church leaders and churches.[2]

The unchurched aren't staying away from church because they think it is boring or irrelevant, at least not anymore. Their lack of confidence isn't directed against God or the Bible; it is with the church and its leaders. In the seeker age, the church tried to make its teachings and its services more user-friendly, practical, and accessible, and to market them to the unchurched. In the post-seeker age Future

Churches are not as concerned with marketing services for unbelievers or entertaining believers as they are in ushering people, believers and unbelievers alike, into the presence of God. Intentionally, they do not water down their teachings or ratchet down the intensity of a service to make it more appealing to unbelievers.

Future Churches did not make this shift to attract the unchurched, but it turns out that the unchurched are not so interested in seeker services as they once were and are attracted to the intense worship experiences of Future Churches. At a Barna 2000/2001 seminar, George Barna explained that the unchurched might not respond as positively to a megachurch that sings praise choruses in a seeker-sensitive service as they might to a smaller, more traditional church. His recent research indicated that the unchurched view the ideal church size to be between one hundred and two hundred people; they prefer traditional hymns with contemporary instruments and arrangements. They prefer the hymns because they know some of them. "They've never heard praise and worship choruses," Barna says.

Barna estimated that 15 percent of the unchurched are likely to return to the church in the near future but that they usually come back to church only when they receive a personal invitation. "Only one fourth of the unchurched have been invited [to a church service]," Barna says. "Among all unchurched adults, just 4 percent were invited and attended church." The "sit back and wait for them to come" approach or send them impersonal invitations via the mail approach may not work in the future. According to Barna, when they return, they don't expect the church to put on a show for them. They want to observe the church being who it genuinely is.

"They have to sense the presence of God," he continued. "They know there is something significant about the presence of God." The trends are pointing away from seeker services. "The primary objective of seeker services is not to expose them to the presence of God," Barna says. "Experiencing God does change people."[3]

Ron Martoia, the founding pastor of Westwinds Community Church in Jackson, Michigan, affirms Barna's findings. He says that the fundamental reason people return to church is that they have experienced God in a service and find the experience so compelling they want to investigate further. "Most people don't return because of great talk, music, media, or art. Those are merely vehicles; they come back because of a deeply moving experience with God."

Without its spiritual core the Future Church is nothing more than an innovative iteration of business as usual. In his book *Morph: The Texture of Leadership for Tomorrow's Church*, Martoia writes: "The craving to experience the transcendent is God-designed. When the church fails to provide an engaging experience of God, then the seeking individual has no choice but to seek filling that God-shaped void in other ways. Far from us buckling to 'consumer demands,' we're raising the need to return to biblical models of experiential encounter so those looking will find."[4]

People don't want to experience church. They want to experience God's presence. The Future Church's battle cry is a return to biblical spirituality, one that is rooted in guiding others to experience God's presence. In the post-seeker age there is no viable alternative to becoming spiritual. "The churches that will cease to exist are not those that are doctrinally errant, but those that are spiritually errant," says Erwin McManus, the lead pastor of Mosaic, in Los Angeles, California. "You can't get away with it anymore. You can't just talk about what the Bible says. You'd better flesh it out, or you are dead. It's not about structures, strategies, programs, or patterns. If you don't rediscover the apostolic, you'll die!"

The church must live what we say we believe. We must "flesh out" our faith. "There is a difference between knowing the good news and being the good news," says Dieter Zander, church planter in San Francisco. "We are the evidence! Everything counts—all the time. With previous generations, a strong preacher could give a good message—even if the church was hypocritical and critical—and people would still get saved. But not anymore."

Biblical spirituality is not another version of the pop spirituality of our age or a new strategy for reaching the unchurched. It is the life and breath of the church. It is its future.

"Moving with the Spirit"
Mosaic, Los Angeles, California

As we walked down the stairs, I held on to the rail while my eyes adjusted from the bright Los Angeles summer sun to the darkened room. Hanging from the ceiling was one of those *Saturday Night*

PORTRAIT

Fever reflector balls. At the back was a mirrored wall with the different colored bottles on the glass shelves. Elevated tables and chairs surrounded the dance floor, and several living room settings flanked the outer walls. *Hmm, I thought, this is what a nightclub looks like.*

The crowd meandered in. Some sat on the floor, others on the permanent furnishings. Some stood. But most of the three-hundred-plus in attendance sat in chairs on the dance floor. This was the first time my wife and I had ever been in a nightclub, but surprisingly we felt right at home. We weren't there to drink or dance. We were there to worship the Creator God with the people of Mosaic. Mosaic had four services every weekend that drew twelve hundred people a week. At the time, three of their services were in their church building on Brady Street, and one was in Soho, a nightclub in downtown Los Angeles.

Erwin McManus, lead pastor at Mosaic, was born in San Salvador, Central America, and raised in Miami. During his college years he was on a philosophical quest for truth. He was an atheist part of the time, an agnostic some of the time, and uncertain the rest of the time. In the midst of his quest, something broke through and shattered his disbelief: God revealed himself to him. Under the ministry of Jim Henry and the First Baptist Church of Orlando, Florida, McManus surrendered to the lordship of Jesus Christ and answered a call to ministry.

McManus moved to the Dallas-Fort Worth Metroplex to enroll in Southwestern Baptist Theological Seminary and continue his ministry there. He was convinced that if the message of Jesus were true, it would work in the worst situations, so he focused his efforts among the urban poor. He and his wife Kim worked side jobs to support their ministry among the people no one wanted—drug dealers, prostitutes, and the homeless. While still in seminary, he traveled to California for a week as part of an evangelistic team. He was hooked. He wanted to return to California.

God's Timing

McManus shared his burden for California at a prayer meeting at Wedgewood Baptist Church. "God is telling me to go to California, and I don't know how or why." A member of the group responded: "I just got a call from Monty McWhorter, the director of Summer Evangelism Teams in California. He needs preachers to come and speak in California churches this summer." That night McManus talked to McWhorter, and within an hour he had an invitation to go to California for the summer.

One summer evening, as he drove from Los Angeles to San Diego, God spoke to him through the city lights. He felt God saying, "Come give your life to the city." God called McManus to believe Deuteronomy 2:36: "There was no city that was too high for us; the Lord our God delivered all over to us" [NASB]. When the summer was over, McManus returned to seminary and his ministry among the urban poor, but in his heart he knew he would be back.

About the same time God was at work in George Luke's family. (George is the owner of the nightclub where Urban Mosaic meets.) His mother-in-law was dying. Searching for comfort, she opened a Bible that a missionary from mainland China gave her years before, "happenchance" to the story of Hezekiah. After reading the story, she asked her daughter Susan what it meant. Overcome with emotion, Susan said, "You're going to live fifteen more years." Of course that was a comforting word to her mother, but she had another question: "What's the second half of the promise mean, 'that you'll be a salvation to the city'?" That was a question Susan couldn't answer. And she wouldn't know the answer to it for fourteen more years.

After ten years in the Dallas Metroplex, McManus packed up his family and moved to Los Angeles and continued his ministry as a futurist and consultant to various Christian ministries. Tom Wolf, pastor of the Church on Brady, had previously asked McManus to consider becoming the pastor of his church. McManus said no. "Anybody who reads anything that Lyle Schaller has written," McManus says, "knows you don't follow a twenty-five-year pastorate because you're destined for failure." He did agree, however, to serve the church as a consultant one day a week after he arrived in LA.

Later the elders of the church approached McManus with the same question. This time McManus said he would become their pastor if he got a unanimous call. Knowing that no pastor gets a unanimous call in a Southern Baptist church, McManus felt safe. When the votes were counted, there wasn't a single one dissenting. After a period of transition, McManus became the pastor of the church, and Wolf moved into a position with Golden Gate Baptist Theological Seminary in Mill Valley.

With a passion he learned serving the urban poor, McManus built on the mission spirit of the Church on

Brady to lead the people into the future. He changed the ambiance of the worship center to feel more like a café than an auditorium. Sprinkled among the traditional seating, they set up mosaic tables and sofas and chairs.

Another thing he changed was their name. An artist creates a mosaic by taking pieces of broken and fragmented glass and arranging them to make a beautiful design that is most attractive when light shines through it. The name *Mosaic* is a metaphor that describes their church. God, the master artist, has placed broken and fragmented people together to form a work of art that is made even more beautiful when the light of Jesus Christ shines through it. Like other metaphors, this metaphor has many nuances. Their church has many shapes and colors in it. The church is multiethnic, multigenerational, and multicultural. Among the hundred-plus people a year the church baptizes are communists, Buddhists, Hindus, and members of the gay community. The church attracts Asians, Hispanics, Anglos, Blacks, and just about any other ethnicity that lives in the area. They shatter the homogeneous unit principle and include everyone. The most frequent criticism McManus hears about the name comes from those who see it as a reference to the Mosaic law. He just tells critics, "The Mosaic law is a historical declaration that God reveals himself to us and that true religion is our response of humility to his initiative." He doesn't mind the connection at all.

To understand this church, traditional Christians need to stand back a little, as they would if they were viewing a mosaic, to really appreciate it, especially if they ever want to understand why one of their services is in a nightclub.

McManus continued to hear the cry of the city. He wasn't satisfied with getting the city into the church; he wanted to get the church into the city, so he went looking for property in the business districts. He found a perfect location that was for sale, but it was ten million dollars out of reach. When they heard that someone had purchased the property, McManus and one of his elders made an appointment to talk to the new owner, George Luke. McManus didn't waste any time in the meeting. He looked Luke straight in the eye and said, "We want to invoke the presence of the living God in this nightclub and make it the center of hope for this entire city."

Luke didn't know what to say. He went home and told his wife Susan about the strange meeting he had with a pastor. When he told her what McManus said about invoking the presence of the living God in the nightclub and making it the center of hope for this entire city, she suddenly understood what the second half of Hezekiah's promise meant, "that you'll be a salvation to the city." The first half of the promise was being fulfilled. Her mother was in her fourteenth year. And now Susan understood how God would fulfill the second half of the promise. This time Luke called McManus. "We've decided to let you use the nightclub," he said. "Could you pay one hundred dollars a week for cleanup?" For the first two months, McManus spent Sunday evenings "spiritually cleansing" the nightclub and invoking God's presence in the place. When he opened the door, people responded to his invitation to come and worship the Creator God—in a nightclub.

When McManus came to the Church on Brady, it was contemporary, following a 1980s model of ministry. In fact, it had been a leader in the contemporary church movement. But even though it was a contemporary church, it was time-locked in the 1980s. Los Angeles had moved into the future while Brady remained behind. Any church with fixed structure in a fluid environment will become outdated and irrelevant. What the church was calling "contemporary" wasn't. So McManus began leading them into the future.

Mosaic's services are definitely in the twenty-first century. The music ranges from "Santana smooth" to the distinctive sounds of "urban alternative." Worship leaders weave drama, music, dance, and MTV-style video clips into the texture of the service. In the audience artists are working on sculptures and paintings while McManus speaks. "I'm committed to Mosaic becoming a place where creativity erupts from every level, from every person," says McManus. Witnessing the creative process helps put the audience in the frame of mind to hear the message. McManus sits on a stool for part of the delivery, but he stands most of the time and preaches his prepared message without notes. The sermons are biblically based with a radical flair. "Our message isn't based on 'felt need.' The driving texture isn't how-tos. Most of our messages are calls to revolution—to turn the world upside down. LA inhales the nations, and it can exhale the gospel. We're here for no less reason than to impact the entire planet. If we capture LA, we will capture the ears of all the nations."

Obviously, Mosaic isn't a "McChurch," but neither is it Church-Lite. The standards for membership are high.

According to McManus, "You can't join our church unless you are willing to live a holy life, be actively involved in ministry, have an evangelistic lifestyle, and at minimum tithe."

What Mosaic is doing isn't about innovation, technology, intelligence, or strategy. McManus explains, "It is really about putting our hearts next to the heart of God and feeling his heartbeat and doing what he wants. Then everybody calls it creativity, innovation, and strategy, but we know deep down inside that we're just moving with the Spirit and presence of God."

And that's the church's future.

Going Vertical

"Pastor, we've really got to start pushing church camp. We've spent a lot of money renting the cabin, and if you don't push it, we won't have anybody come."

"We need to recruit people for the church choir. The participation is going down, but if you'd say something from the pulpit, I'm sure it would help."

"We're starting a new class in Discipleship Training. Can you promote it today?"

"Why didn't you say anything about the mission offering this morning? People aren't going to give if you don't say something!"

I heard these four questions from different church leaders on the same Sunday morning. Not, "Pastor, we've been praying for a unique visitation from the Lord today and that God would use you as an anointed vessel." Not, "I couldn't wait to come to church today to stand together with you in the presence of the Lord." But, "Can you use the limited time you have to speak to God's people to promote something I care deeply about?" On one level I sympathize with their concern for their ministries and their enthusiasm to promote them. But on another level, when I reflect on their questions, I start to feel the way I did when I was a college student, sitting in my boss's office.

When I was in college, I worked at a furniture store on the delivery crew during the week and on the sales staff on Saturdays. One afternoon the owner of the store called me into his office for a chat to talk about my future with the company. He had plans of moving me on the permanent sales force, which would have been a good deal for me. But before he made the change, he wanted to discuss a few things with me. "What church are you going to?" he asked. *Cool,* I thought, *he's concerned about my spiritual condition.* "I go to College Heights Baptist Church," I replied.

In a million years I couldn't have guessed what he was about to say. He cocked his head to the right, looked off into the distance, as though he was deep in thought. He stroked his chin a few times, then turned back to look me straight in the eye. "First Baptist is a larger church and thought of more highly in the business community. I think it would be good if you'd start going to church there. It would be good for business." I didn't say a word. Perhaps he took my silence as an understood compliance, but if he did, he misunderstood me. I wasn't about to prostitute a worship service for my personal gain. Deep down inside I knew it was wrong to use a worship service to promote a furniture store. Worship has a higher purpose.

Yet there have been times when I felt that was exactly what I was doing since becoming a pastor—not promoting a furniture store but promoting a business just the same. Yes, it is the one time when the most people are in the same room, and it makes great logistical sense to take advantage of that time to promote the ministries of the church or the church itself. But is promotion worship? No, I'm not concerned about announcements per se. I know that, in moderation, they are a necessary part of the service. But I am concerned about the mentality that views the gathering of the people together as an opportunity to build something. Even if what we are building is the Lord's work, can't that mentality turn the worship service into an infomercial?

Sometimes the pressure I feel to become an infomercial host doesn't come from without. It comes from within, especially when I succumb to the temptation to impress "church shoppers." The pressure is self-imposed. No one would say, "Now Pastor, I've got some friends coming this week, so you'd better put in a little extra time on the sermon and make sure the service runs smoothly." This demon is my own. It isn't a church program I feel like I have to promote—it is the church itself. And to my shame I'll have to admit that more than once I've been more concerned about what a prospective member thought about a worship service than what God thought.

"If you'll join our church, not only will you get a well-educated pastor who is thoughtful, caring, and dynamic, but we'll throw in a choir that blesses you with their anthems and a youth program that will keep your teenagers off drugs and out of your hair." Is that the purpose of a worship service? Should I really try impressing "church shoppers" so they'll come back to the church instead of going to a church down the street with a better pastor, programs, or facilities? Whether I am trying to please a church leader who wants me to promote a program or to impress a prospective church member enough to return, there is a problem. The service has become horizontal—primarily concerned with what people think. To sum it up, that's the whole problem with a horizontal orientation in worship. It asks, "What do people think?" instead of "What does God think?" In horizontal worship those on the stage are the actors, the people are the audience, and God is a distant observer.

Prostitution

Mark Driscoll, pastor of Mars Hill Fellowship in Seattle, calls this mentality "raping American consumerism." He describes it this way: "Churches are competing against each other, trying to gain a larger market share. Since the customer is always right, these churches do market research, discover their target, then advertise to members of the target audience and service their needs. It is prostitution, turning the church into whatever the market demands it to be." *Prostitution* is a strong word. But if a church ceases to teach what it is supposed to teach just so it can attract more people, the word may not be strong enough. Are we living in the time Paul described in 2 Timothy 4:3? "For the time will come when men will not put up with sound doctrine. Instead, to suit their own desires, they will gather around them a great number of teachers to say what their itching ears want to hear" (NIV).

In all fairness the contemporary church didn't tilt the church to a horizontal orientation; before the seeker movement, the traditional church was already horizontal. The traditional church's focus was on believers' spiritual needs and curiosity. Great Bible teachers emerged who made the deep truths of the Scripture understandable. Churches distinguished themselves from one another by their stands on theological issues and used their worship services to teach their particular views and show why they were "right" and everyone else was "wrong." In some ways the traditional church was living out another passage in 2 Timothy: "Ever learning, and never able to come to the knowledge of the truth" (2 Tim. 3:7 KJV).

When I was in high school, I met a girl at the drive-in movie theater and asked her out on a date. She agreed to go out with me but said her church was in revival so we'd have to go after the service. Innocently, I suggested that we go to the revival first and then get something to eat. A big mistake! She had no way of knowing, but the guest preacher spent the evening explaining why the Baptists were wrong and the Churches of Christ were right. At the end of the worship service, she was embarrassed, and I felt more than a little uncomfortable. The service was hostile. But in all fairness the same thing could have happened in reverse. Baptist churches and Churches of Christ have their differences and in those days that's what they talked about when they got together. And it wasn't just a denominational thing. Even within the same groups, issues such as eschatology, predestination, and gifts divided people. This approach did not resonate with non-Christians, who didn't care about the issues, understand the terminology, or have a background to interpret the ritual. To them church was boring, dry, and irrelevant. But that really didn't matter to the traditional churches because these churches weren't really trying to attract nonbelievers; their services were geared to believers who agreed with them. Occasionally, a church would have evangelistic meetings and encourage the congregation to invite their "lost friends." The mood was a full-throttle, Bible-thumping turn-or-burn, we're-right-and-you're-wrong, aggressive sales pitch. The church thought that if the preacher could only convince lost people to believe what the Christians believe, then they would become Christians, too.

Sometimes the tilt toward the believers was so obvious that we were downright rude. When I first started pastoring, if any strangers were in the audience, I'd ask them to stand up and introduce themselves to the congregation. The ushers would give them a card that asked for personal information with a red ribbon that could detach from the card for them to put on their lapel so everyone would know they were visiting and could greet them. At the time I thought we were being friendly, but today I think we were incredibly rude. What a way to treat a guest! We not only put them in a roomful of strangers, using a language that only the initiated could understand, but we also asked them to stand up and speak. Then we asked them for information that was nobody's business and put a lame red ribbon on their lapel so they would stand out like the sore thumb we made them.

Courtesy

In a strong reaction to the believer orientation of the traditional church, the contemporary church shifted the target of the worship service from the believer to the nonbeliever. In many ways it was a needed correction. The church isn't a private club "for members only." The seeker movement reminded the church that our visitors should be treated as honored guests. There should be signs that direct traffic, greeters that provide logistical information, clean restrooms, comfortable rooms, adequate child care; and the services should be user-friendly. These corrections were needed, but the seeker movement didn't change the horizontal orientation of the service at all; all it did was change the target from believers to nonbelievers. If all that has happened in the last twenty years is that preachers can wear polo shirts rather than a suit, that we sing short songs (contemporary choruses) instead of long songs (hymns), and that the atmosphere is casual instead of formal, what was really accomplished? Yes, I'll be the first to agree that the services shouldn't have been believer-focused, but neither do I think they should be seeker-focused. Worship services should be God-focused. We need to go vertical!

Looking Up

When we gather for worship, we stand beside one another in the presence of God. We are the actors, and God is the audience. Our focus should be on him. God's holy

Word is not a book of principles for successful living; it is a powerful revelation of redemption, grace, and reconciliation. We don't gather to promote a program or the church; we gather to worship. And when we do, we express our brokenness before God. "Woe is me," Isaiah said. We experience grace and celebrate redemption. In song, in dance, in readings, in laughter, through tears, we brush up against the grandeur of God. And when we do, we are changed. "Here am I," Isaiah said, "send me." Believers and nonbelievers alike need that experience.

A church with a vertical orientation isn't formal or casual. It is intense. Sally Morganthaller, author of *Worship Evangelism* says, "Worship is fully divine. The church doesn't need to make any apologies for the spiritual content and activity of the worship service. The worship service is also fully human. We ask people to respond to the divine with their right and left brains, with all their senses, and out of their reality."

It isn't about whether the church uses a praise band or a choir, sings old songs or new ones, dresses up or dresses down. That stuff is all window dressing. A church can use whatever liturgy it chooses. That isn't the point. The point is that worship is all about God. It isn't about the way people dress or what style of music they like. The key question is, Are they going horizontal, or are they going vertical?

That shift changes the moment worship leaders understand that a worship service has to be a "no-ego zone." Worship leaders need to check their egos at the door. How else can God be the focus? Worshippers need their leaders to have the spirit of John the Baptist when he said, "He must increase, but I must decrease" (John 3:30 KJV). It isn't about the singers who hold the microphone or the actors who are in the sketch or the preacher in the pulpit or the instrumentalists in the band. All these people are important but only as a medium that enables the worshipper to experience God. But neither is it about the believer or seeker in the audience. Worship is about God who is on his throne.

Making sure it stays that way begins by understanding that the place of worship is a no-ego zone, but it also includes awareness that there believers and nonbelievers are present. That doesn't mean the church must exclude meaningful ritual, but it does mean that the leaders must explain what they are asking the congregation to do and why they are asking them to do it.

"While connecting with 'the holy' is the focus of worship," says Ron Martoia, "we need to use language that the uninitiated can understand, but we challenge them with the awesome power of God and allow them to navigate that instead of using all their energy to decipher practices and language they don't understand." Rituals are important but not when they become routine. "Rituals are acts of the past, conducted in the present with life-giving meaning," says Mark Driscoll. "Routine is doing what we've always done because it's been here a while."

It isn't about the elements of worship either. In the Future Church the human elements of worship include ambiance, music, art, dance, drama, film clips, preaching, solitude, reflection, silence, and ritual. Those elements help the worshipper respond to the divine. All of those elements can be present, but the church may still miss the mark if it doesn't have a vertical orientation. But going full-tilt vertical will transform the lives of those who are present, believers and unbelievers alike, because we all need God and we all need to worship him.

"Vintage Christianity"

Clusters of people form a maze in the hallways. Some are on their way home after attending the six o'clock service; others are just arriving for the eight o'clock service. Their laughter and con-

versation emit electricity into the air. Inside, the curtains to the elevated stage are closed, and portable black curtains surround the perimeter of the large auditorium to give the space an intimate feel. A smaller, temporary stage sits in front on the same level as the audience with one large PowerPoint screen directly above it and another one on either side of it. The room is dark, giving context for the candles and the images on the screen.

At Graceland, worship begins the moment you walk in the room. The service is earthy, with plenty of room for worshippers to respond to God's movement. It contains two or three worship sets that feature hymns, original songs, and new releases. Most of the music is loud and celebrative, but some of it is melancholy and pensive. There is space to celebrate God's grace and mercy in community, but there is also freedom to encounter God in solitude. Worship leader Josh Fox says, "At some point in the night, I like to have a time where people can just confess stuff." Sometimes the confession takes place in a thick silence—not an awkward, self-conscious silence but a silence where the gentle breeze of God's voice speaks. At times it is easy to forget that anyone else is present—anyone, that is, except God. Some worshippers stand before God's presence. Others sit in their chairs and quietly bow their heads. Still others walk behind the curtains and go into their private "prayer closet" where they are free to be expressive—to bow, sometimes literally, before a holy God.

What makes Graceland unique isn't the PowerPoint, the music, the art, the candles, or the curtains. It isn't the techniques or the ambiance. It is its spiritual essence. And it begins with the pastor.

When Dan Kimball, the pastor of the Graceland church services at Santa Cruz Bible Church, walks to the microphone, he seems like just another guy. He could be any one of the people in attendance. And it's not just his casual dress. A preacher can be condescending in a golf shirt as easily as he can in a suit. It's his humble persona. He's a peer preacher, a man preaching to his peers.

Maybe it's because of his journey. A "Jesus freak" witnessed to Kimball on the streets in New Jersey in the late 1970s. "You're going to hell and will perish in a lake of fire if you don't repent," the man said. Kimball had never heard that before. As a child, his mother did drop him off at a Dutch Reformed church, the same one George Washington attended, but Kimball never really paid attention. He knelt with the street preacher and received Christ. But Kimball didn't attend church until he graduated from college and started going to a small church in London while playing in a 1980s rockabilly punk band. Because he didn't have a church background, Kimball didn't understand the church terminology the pastor used, but under the influence of the Bible his life began to change. A year later he was baptized in the Jordan River. After Kimball's band folded, he headed off to Israel to see the land of the Bible. He joined a kibbutz, picking grapefruit in the mornings for five dollars a week plus room and board. The rest of the day belonged to him, and he spent it reading his Bible and exploring the lands he read about. Later he attended Bible college and seminary, but he spent his formative years in a self-guided, spiritual quest. Kimball relates to his audience. He was one of them. He is one of them.

Or maybe it's because of his philosophy. In many churches pastors look and act like businessmen, not spiritual "holy men." In his January/February 2002 column for *Rev* magazine, Kimball contrasted the persona of the Christian pastor with Buddhist priests. "As pastors we talk of our busy schedules and proudly carry our cell phones, Palm Pilots, and laptops, often using modern business lingo to describe church ministry," Kimball says. "And we sure do like using business titles to describe our pastoral roles—such as 'executive pastor,' 'senior pastor,' 'associate pastor,' and 'director of ministries.'"

In contrast with the pastor's ethos, people often describe Buddhist leaders as "holy men." When the Dalai Lama, the exiled Tibetan Buddhist leader, visited the Bay area recently, Kimball observed people's reaction to him. Schoolchildren described him as "a man of love and peace." Local college students called him "a wise and holy man." Parents brought their children to hear him speak because they said he is "one of the last living symbols of purity and goodness."[5] Unfortunately, many churches are better known for their organization and efficiency than their spirituality. Don't get me wrong. There's nothing wrong with being organized, but there *is* something wrong with being spiritually deficient.

The Christian message is inherently spiritual. It will be well received by a generation seeking a spiritual experience. That's why the church must not strip the message of its spiritual essence. "Isn't church the place where people meet God?" Kimball asks. "The Future Church is raw—'Here's Jesus. We're here to worship him.' Emerging generations are looking for spirituality and expect a spiritual experience in a church. We don't have to hide what we are doing anymore. This is a post-seeker age. It's back to the basics." It is "Vintage Christianity."

Unplugged

Until the mid-1990s, Santa Cruz Bible Church was doing a full-throttle youth event with high-energy music, colored lights, disco ball, video clips—the works. For the longest time it was effectively reaching unchurched youth, but by the mid-1990s mostly Christian kids were coming, and when they graduated from high school, they weren't coming to church anymore. The youth leadership began experimenting during the summers, trying to find a way to reach the emerging generations. After exploring several options, they decided to go "unplugged." They darkened the room, lit some candles, and arranged the chairs in a circle, creating a more "spiritual" environment. The teens, churched and unchurched alike, responded positively to the approach.

Times were changing. During the seeker era churches were trying to overcome the idea that church was boring and Christianity was irrelevant, so a stage-driven, entertainment-based liturgy emerged. In the post-seeker era, the typical unchurched person doesn't think church is boring; most don't have a clue what church is because they've never been. But they do have an idea who Christians are, and that idea is mostly negative. Recently Graceland interviewed several students at University of California Santa Cruz and asked them, "What comes to your mind when you hear the word *Jesus?*" They had great comments such as "beautiful," "wonderful," "good teacher." Then the interviewers asked the students, "What do you think about Christians?" They responded, "They are angry," and "Always blaming people for things." Everything they said was negative.

Changing times demand changing methods. Instead of putting on a "big show" to entertain the youth, the church was learning that they needed to introduce them to the basics of the faith in a raw, stripped-down, spiritual environment. They knew they were on to something but didn't know what they should do next. Should they plant a new church? Or should they start something within the church that would target the age group that was dropping out of the church? After discussion and prayer, in the fall of 1996, SCBC replaced the church's college ministry with Graceland. Graceland wasn't a church; it was the church services of Santa Cruz Bible Church (SCBC) for the emerging culture. They didn't use the phrase "a church within a church" to describe who they were because that would imply that there are two bodies within one body—a theological impossibility. The average person who attended Santa Cruz Bible Church's other services probably would describe Graceland as the services where a lot of young people attend—a fairly accurate description. But it is more than that. Specifically, Graceland targeted people from eighteen to thirty who wouldn't normally attend the other services of SCBC but who would relate to the texture of Graceland. Attendance exploded.

Within a year Graceland grew to around two hundred and was expanding beyond its "college ministry" boundaries. When some teens and adults over thirty started attending, they began to learn that the issue wasn't so much a specific age group as a specific mind-set—a postmodern worldview. So what should they do? Should they "card" people at the door and turn them away if they didn't fit the initial profile? Or should they welcome whoever came? A year after Graceland began as a college ministry, it became a church service and opened its doors to people of all ages. They began offering communion, baptizing their converts, and receiving offerings. A little over a year later, the service grew to the point that they had to move it from the chapel into the main auditorium, and a year later they went to two services. Graceland's services had a distinct personality, but they had the same doctrine, elders, and ministries as the Santa Cruz Bible Church. Gracelanders are a part of SCBC and join with those who attend the other services to minister to their church family, their community, and their world. All are definitely one church.

Reaching the Young, Respecting the Elders

Dan Kimball says, "So many younger churches miss out on the older mentoring the younger. What works well with our being part of Santa Cruz Bible Church is that there are people who lead our small groups who don't attend Graceland; they love having the young people in their homes. This is a critical thing that the church as a whole needs to do because we've become so compartmentalized."

In many ways Kimball stands between two generations. Definitely he has a passion to reach the emerging generations, but he loves and respects his elders too. Hanging on his office wall are the pictures of three elderly men, placed side-by-side, and mounted in a single frame. On the left is Stuart Allen, the eighty-three-year-old pastor in England who gave Dan his introduction into church life; in the middle is ninety-year-old Dr. Mitchell, the founder of Multnomah who met with Dan every week while Dan attended seminary; and on the right is his eighty-year-old father-in-law, Rod Clendenen, who met with Dan every Wednesday night in a mentoring role when Dan first starting attending SCBC.

"These are guys who made it through their entire lives," Kimball says. "They finished well. We need to be honoring people with gray hair more. We're so into just promoting the young, but what about people who walked with God their whole lives?"

Yes, Graceland is predominately younger, but because it is a part of SCBC, Gracelanders are able to interact with other generations in the church's ministries and in their small groups. "Our home groups are assigned by age, but the leaders are intentionally older," Kimball says. "When relationships are made, people will hang out together."

New Beginnings

But then in November 2003 Graceland closed their doors forever to give way to a new church that would meet at the same time in the same space with the same pastors but as a sister church to SCBC, not a service of the church. On January 11, 2004, Vintage Faith Church (VFC) was born. It isn't Graceland with a new name and organization, according to Kimball. VFC blends a mix of the ancient and the future, bringing life and meaning to some practices of ancient liturgy. They are also forming a choir to assist Fox in leading worship. The choir will do ancient choral hymns, spirituals, and gospel music. Eventually, the church plans to offer services in different locations with different "feels." As soon as possible they plan on opening a location on the west side of town as another "large gathering location," and a downtown location that will have a coffeehouse ambiance and will be "Santa Cruz funky."

"I like the concept of diverse worship experiences in a church," Kimball says. "You could have a worship service that is hymns and organ for people who are drawn to that, but that is just a small part of what the church is." The church is much more than that; it is more than styles and preferences and textures of services. Kimball says, "We overestimate the value of putting on a really cool, funky weekend thing. We can have nine hundred people there, but that doesn't mean it is authentic [worship]." Worship isn't a performance or a techno-demonstration. It is connecting with God. It is a spiritual experience. "It's not whether we are using art in the service. It is whether we are making disciples," Kimball says. Really, the church is much more than its services. "We are placing more value on what happens during the week—things like how many people are in home groups, how many go down and feed the homeless on Friday nights, and how many come to the prayer meetings."

Vintage Faith is a place where people enter a community and encounter God's love in others, where they experience God through worship, explore truth in the Scriptures, and express their faith to the world around them. It isn't "cool" Christianity, "techno" Christianity or artsy Christianity; it is "vintage Christianity." "We need to be heartbroken over people, and we need to weep for them and educate other Christians to do the same," Kimball says. "Hopefully, we're creating a culture where people can fall in love with God and his Word and are developing disciples who are 'self-feeders,' going deep into the Word, saturating their mind with its pages, and embodying its teachings to the world. People who pray. People who are really in love with God."

At VFC, they are calling on their people to be holy—to be "Vintage" Christians.

www.thefuturechurch.com

Conventional wisdom says that emerging generations lack real purpose and are drifting through life. They've become cynical, not really believing that anything can make society—or their souls—whole again. What is the church's response?

Fulcrum Point 3

Get Radical

There was a time when America's Christianized culture helped keep a church afloat in a community. I grew up in a state that had "blue laws," laws that prohibited stores from selling nonessential items on Sunday in order to discourage shopping on the Lord's Day. Our school district had a policy against football practice going past six o'clock on Wednesday evenings because it might keep players from attending prayer meeting at their church. We not only had school prayer; we had school worship services. When a local church was in revival, the school would open the assembly hall to the evangelist to speak to the high school students during school hours.

Not everyone was a Christian, but the culture was Christianized. Going to church was the accepted thing to do. Not going could jeopardize a person's standing in the community as well as his or her business relationships with members of the Christian community. Businesses offered deep discounts or provided complimentary goods and services to the church. Today, attending church isn't the cultural norm, though twenty-first-century people are deeply spiritual. But their spirituality does not necessarily resemble biblical spirituality. Some spiritually curious people are as likely to attend a pagoda, a temple, or a mosque as a church. But they aren't automatically monogamous to any one religion. Like passing through a cafeteria line, people pick and choose elements out of different religions they will follow. It isn't "no faith" or a "different faith." It is "designer faith."

When we eat out, I've noticed that we tend to ask for substitutions. We ask for a salad instead of fries or fruit instead of hash browns. We don't go back to restaurants that forbid substitutions or charge us extra for them. We want it the way we want it, and we don't want to be limited by the menu. Do we expect to have it our way with faith too? In his *Newsweek* article "The Changing Face of the Church," Kenneth Woodward writes: "In India, where sin is identified with bad karma in this and previous lives, many converts interpret the cross to mean that Jesus' self-sacrifice removes their own karmic deficiencies, thus liberating their souls from future rebirths."[1] Can a person be Hindu and Christian at the same time? No. But Hinduism and Christianity can be blended to meet spiritual needs. In reality, isn't that what the New Age movement is—the blending of Christianity with something else?

The only hope the church has to reach people in this spiritualized culture is with the life-transforming, radical power of the gospel. Paul wrote, "For I am not ashamed of the gospel, for it is the power of God for salvation to everyone who believes, to the Jew first and also to the Greek" (Rom. 1:16 NASB). The gospel has explosive power to transform people's lives and to make the church a radical force in the culture. "That's what's exciting about the world in which we live," says Erwin McManus, lead pastor of Mosaic. "Only the viable church of Jesus Christ will survive, the inauthentic need not apply. I want to live in the world where, if the church is not the revolution that Jesus died to establish two thousand years ago, it ceases to exist. I want to live in a world where the church has no more crutches or buffers to guard her from injury. I want a church where a culture no longer protects her. Whenever the gospel enters an environment, it prevails."

Future Churches are answering a call to revolution— a call to a radical Christian lifestyle that depends on the power of the gospel to transform lives and to propel the church.

"Fishing Expedition"
Quest 419, Tampa Bay, Florida

Like David in Saul's armor, the vestments of the Lutheran clergy didn't quite fit Chris Kratzer. Part of it was the formality and ritualism; part of it was the theology;

PORTRAIT

and part of it was the traditional/liturgical approach to ministry.

And then there were the conflicts. After spending a couple of years as an associate pastor, Chris accepted his first senior pastorate in 1998 at Atonement Lutheran Church in Wesley Chapel, Florida. Atonement was a traditional church that wanted to become more contemporary, so they turned to Chris, a young minister acquainted with the contemporary church movement. Feeling he had a mandate for change from the congregation, Kratzer put a team together that established three types of services—a traditional/ liturgical service, an "Amy Grant" service, and a contemporary service. It is one thing for a church to say they want change and another for them to embrace it. And Atonement definitely didn't embrace it. "The problem wasn't that these changes didn't work," Kratzer says. "The problem was that they *did*."

"One of the most disheartening things is when God's blessing becomes threatening to the church," Kratzer says. "When more people started coming, wanting ownership, people started complaining." One time a parishioner told him, "Chris, I've noticed some new people coming to church, and I don't see them as the kind of people me and my husband can be friends with. And I'm not so sure if you should be spending so much time with them." Kratzer couldn't believe that he was arguing with someone about whether reaching people was the primary goal of the church. "The church people saw the unchurched as the enemy instead of people to reach," Kratzer says.

As his discontent in the congregation was growing, so was his uneasiness with the state of Lutheran theology. "In Lutheran circles, there is a cheap grace—everybody is going to heaven no matter what you believe or do," Kratzer says. "I couldn't stand up as a pastor and buy into the allowance of homosexuality, infant baptism, and that stuff."

Conversion

Kratzer had settled on his vocation before he came to faith in Christ and selected the Lutheran church by default. When his pastor recommended he consider going into the ministry, it made a lot of sense to Chris. After all, he was as moral as the next guy, and his friends were always turning to him for advice. He liked the idea of helping people and of being someone important. So he headed off to college to become a Lutheran minister. His plan was to spend his undergraduate years focusing on developing his musical skills, then go to seminary to learn how to be a pastor. On the surface everything looked fine, but deep inside he knew something was missing. He was seeking credentials to become a pastor, but he wasn't walking with the Lord. He wasn't even attending church. But there was no pressure from the institutions he attended to get his act together. During his senior year Chris flew to a Lutheran seminary he wanted to attend to check it out. While he was there, the seminary sponsored an Octoberfest party, complete with a keg of beer for the students and prospective students.

The thrust of his training was academic and psychological. After four years of college and three years of seminary, he knew the Bible inside and out, could help a parishioner get in touch with his inner child, and comfort the grieving. But it was all mechanical. During his final year of seminary, Kratzer became dissatisfied with his duplicity and struggled through his own "dark night of the soul." In that season of spiritual warfare, God convicted him of his sinfulness, and Kratzer placed his trust in Jesus Christ to save his soul. "I invited Jesus into my heart and entire life. What had always been in my head opened into my heart as God brought me to my knees," Kratzer says. "It was like a flood came pouring in, and my heart took off. From that point on, my call to ministry took on a whole new shape and essence."

Choices

Kratzer didn't doubt his call to ministry, but he did have a big question looming over his soul: Which ministry? "I wanted the freedom to do ministry and reach people—getting back to the heart of what God's church is. I'm not saying all Lutherans weren't getting it, but I needed to live out God's call in my life," Kratzer says. "God is creative, passionate, and life-changing, and sometimes we lose that in church. We lose the creativity, the passion, and the purpose, and we pursue survival and comfort."

In his disillusionment, while still a Lutheran pastor, he started attending the Friday night service at Crosstown Community Church (a large church affiliated with the Tampa Bay Baptist Association) and meeting with their pastor, Michael Hailey. Soon he and his wife were baptized at Crosstown, even while he was a Lutheran pastor. "It was something Amy and I wanted to do. We just wanted to get that right," Kratzer says. "We knew that somebody from the

Lutheran church I was still pastoring might be there, but we did it anyway."

After leaving Atonement and the Lutheran denomination, Kratzer put his resumé together and interviewed at contemporary churches across the country, hoping to land a staff position. During his quest he searched his own soul for the answer to one question: "What would a church for my unchurched friends look like?" He knew it wouldn't look like the church he was pastoring, but he wasn't so sure it would be a seeker church either. He did a word study of *seek* in the New Testament and found that Jesus always used it in the perfect tense, meaning "to seek and keep on seeking." "It was then that I discovered that for God, reaching out to people isn't a one-time thing. It is a flat-out quest," Kratzer says. Matthew 4:19 became his theme verse: "Come, be my disciples, and I will show you how to fish for people!" (NLT).

It isn't that the unchurched were seekers; it is that the church was supposed to be a seeker—seeking out the lost. A church should be on a quest to reach people, Kratzer concluded. It should be fishing for people. He developed a simple philosophy of ministry: "Helping people come to follow Christ in their life, the epitome of that comes in our ability to fish for others." He felt that believers should be followers of Christ, not just fans—taking following Christ seriously. "It's not about being perfect, but it is about progressing," Kratzer says. "We accept people where they are, but we don't think it is OK to leave them there." When he asked Michael Hailey, senior pastor at Crosstown Community Church, what he thought about his philosophy of ministry, Hailey said, "Chris, you really need to do this."

The Quest

Until that moment Kratzer's intentions weren't to start a church. As he listened to Hailey's encouragement, he realized that what he held in his hands wasn't something to present to an established church so he could get a job; it was the blueprint for a new church start: Quest 419. (The name combines *quest,* a word that captures the perfect tense of the word *seek,* and 419 from Matthew 4:19.) When he announced his intentions to start a new church, some of his former parishioners wanted to go with him. He responded, "Let's take six months and worship together, and let me orient you in what we will be doing." Certainly he wanted to give them an opportunity to be a part of it if that was how God was leading; but in the back of his mind, he knew they might not understand what it was going to mean to be a part of Quest 419. Over the next six months, most of the people realized that though they loved Pastor Chris, this wasn't for them. When it was all said and done, only one family stayed.

Quest 419 wasn't their father's Oldsmobile. "I knew people would buy into the person before they buy into a vision, but the time comes when you have to buy into both. And that time came when they realized that God was calling them into a traditional setting," Kratzer says. He was happy that they discovered God's will for their lives but a little concerned about the stability of the new ministry. He'd taken a lot of financial risk to launch the church: he'd cashed in his pension, and his wife had to take a full-time job and took out an $18,000 personal loan. But he was willing to take the risks to reach people that no one was reaching.

Kratzer says, "Great things happen where our resources end and God's resources begin."

With fewer than a dozen people in the core group, Quest 419 launched their ultracontemporary worship style on December 24, 2000, with twenty-five people in attendance, many of them well-wishers. They met in a double-wide student ministry trailer at another church, the only place they could find. When the dust settled and the well-wishers were gone, there were days when attendance was low. Sometimes it was very low. "One time we had three people come," Kratzer says. "I asked them, do we really want to do this?" He walked to the window of the portable building and prayed, "God, I don't know how you are going to do this." But within a few months they had outgrown the temporary space and needed to get out. But they didn't have a place to go—not until they signed a lease on a seven-thousand-square-foot former auto parts store. The space was a stretch financially, but it was perfect for them.

The people of Quest 419 are specific about their image; they want a club or a coffeehouse feel. The room is dark with lava lamps, glowing televisions, candles, and string lights. In a way it is back-to-the-sixties retro, rather eclectic. The stage lighting includes black lights, theatrical fog machines, and pocket scans; the lighting moves and changes while the band leads in worship. Fifteen or twenty people can sit on couches during the service; they have a café area with a dozen bar stools, and the rest of the seating is around small tables that seat three or four.

The Friday night service usually lasts just over an hour. Sometimes it starts with an original video clip or commercial. At other times it starts with a poetry reading. The band does three or four songs, usually adaptations of current offerings that they make a bit edgier. The service is designed to avoid self-consciousness and increase God-consciousness among the worshippers. "You don't have to void yourself of the clothes you like to wear or your sense of humor to come to church," Kratzer says. During the offering the pastor sometimes does a question-and-answer session with the audience. They write their questions on three-by-five cards, and he spends one minute apiece on up to ten questions.

A spotlight illuminates the pastor as he sits on a stool. His sermons are straightforward, biblical messages. "I can say something that is so 'in their face' during a message, but they will accept it because it is coming from a genuine love and an authentic heart," Kratzer says. "I don't pull any punches, but I am careful how I articulate and create an atmosphere where they can hear it. People want to hear the truth. They are craving it. But they want to hear it in a way they can hear it from a source that has their best interest at heart."

Creating that atmosphere takes intentional effort. "What's attractive about our church isn't any one thing— it is the whole package, the whole approach," Kratzer says. "Doing church in the future is very intentional in the areas of worship, and the images we use as a cultural tool to communicate, in the areas of discipleship and authenticity. It doesn't just haphazardly happen. Some churches are very serious about people being disciples but have no clue about how to communicate that culturally. We are very culturally relevant in our style, but it is serious business." It isn't just about the music or the atmosphere. "We feel that images we put out are just as important as the music we use," Kratzer adds.

God blessed their fishing expedition. Within two years the church grew to just under a hundred a week, 90 percent of them unchurched people. They were still on the edge—what church ever has enough money or volunteers? But they were well on their way to being a viable self-supporting church when Kratzer decided to go on a much-deserved vacation. He returned to a theological controversy that ultimately split the church and left it too wounded to continue. In September 2002, the church had its final worship service celebrating what God had done in their lives, and then they closed the door for good. For Kratzer, compromising on his biblical convictions wasn't an option—even if it meant the ship wouldn't come back from sea.

Not every church plant survives. It is a harsh reality but a reality nonetheless. There are no "guaranteed success formulas," no "three easy steps" or "seven tried-and-proven principles" in post-seeker ministry. The very nature of a radical ministry puts it at greater risk of not surviving than one that plays it safe and caters to convention and sticks with known quantities. Churches that choose not to play it safe, the pioneering churches that go out in uncharted waters, may not all survive; but they leave a legacy for other churches that follow in their wake, benefiting from their successes and learning from their mistakes.

The value of the Future Church is not in its ability to stay in the comfort of safe harbor but to risk going offshore, out of sight of land and risking to save the shipwrecked, drowning lives in our cultural ocean, even if the rescue mission lasts for a short while because their boat was terminally damaged in heavy seas." Kratzer says, "I believe the future of God's church is in the hearts of people who are willing to go on these rescue missions, whether long or short, prestigious or unpopular, safe or secure, to rescue those who have been deemed too far offshore and out of reach. And though my ship has been capsized, this seaman still believes in going offshore, doing what it takes to reach people, and is ready and waiting for my captain's orders."

A few months later Kratzer received those orders and is now the pastor of C-3, a church in North Carolina. He and his wife Amy are in the early stages of their ministry there, excited about this chapter in their lives. God was faithful to them. When they sold their house, their increased equity more than covered the money they'd "sacrificed" for God in planting the church. Once again they count on "great things happening where man's resources end and God's resources begin."

The beginning of God's resources—not a bad place to be. With or without a pension plan.

Transformation

Sitting in a window seat, Roger Williams III was looking forward to thumbing through a magazine on a short flight from Sacramento to attend a national youth ministry conference in San Diego. He'd fastened his seatbelt, made sure his chair was in the full upright position, his tray table locked, and his luggage properly stowed, when two well-dressed Ally McBeal look-alikes sat down next to him. Their conversation competed for attention with his magazine. They talked about the club scene—what they enjoyed drinking, who they were dating, their intimate relationships with men, both single and married. Then it turned into a gripe session.

"Why do guys have such a hard time committing?" one asked. "And why don't they ever leave their wives like they promise to?" another complained. They talked about work for a while, and about the time Williams was tuning out, one of them said, "But you know, if it wasn't for church, my life would really be hell."

By now Williams was only pretending to read his magazine. They had his full attention.

"Wow, you go to church, too. I know exactly how you feel. If it wasn't for church, I don't know where I'd be."

"Yeah, I know what you mean," the other woman said. "If I miss more than two weeks of church, everything in my life goes nuts."

The plane started its descent into San Diego, and everything got quiet. Williams sat still—stunned by what he'd just heard. These women weren't genuine seekers—people looking for the truth. Instead they were going to church to get their religious fix.

These women on the plane didn't need a sermon on five steps to success. They didn't need a Band-Aid. They needed transformation. They were getting a faith inoculation when they needed an antidote for sin. They needed a church that would confront them, not accommodate them. They needed a church that would get past their felt needs and speak to their greatest need, to confess their sin and turn to Christ.

Transformational Teaching

Some churches criticize people behind their backs but never proclaim the transforming power of the gospel to their faces. Other churches try to help people get their lives cleaned up but never ask them to change. Still other churches adapt their methodologies so a person can feel comfortable in church while remaining in his sins. Sinners don't need someone to make them feel bad or make them feel good. They need someone to tell them about Christ, who can transform their lives. No subtleties here. People don't need to learn to be the best they can be in their sin; they need transformation. "[Churches] are in the business to do ministry to facilitate transformation," Barna said at a Barna 2000/2001 Conference. "That is the only reason we exist."[2]

The voice on the road to Damascus didn't coach Saul on how to get along with people of other faiths or how to bring his temper under control. Saul didn't need to master his own destiny by getting in touch with his feelings about the past or rechannel his energy in the present to create a new and brighter future. He needed transformation. The Lord's words to him were direct and in his face: "Saul, Saul, why are you persecuting me?" (Acts 9:4). Saul didn't need coaching or a self-help group; he needed transformation, and that's what he got.

Future Churches aren't interested in teaching self-help lessons; they want to see people's lives transformed. Whereas seeker churches emphasize, "Neither do I condemn you," Future Churches don't stop there; they also say, "Go and sin no more." Sinners don't need a fix. They need a life-changing experience, a transformation like Reuben and Pat got.

The gunshot rang through the school yard. The bullet missed Pat and lodged in the doorpost. Pat ducked into the classroom as Reuben scattered with the rest of the kids. Reuben found a place to stash the gun and went back into class. That night he snuck out of his house, retrieved the gun, and put it back in his family's gun case.

No one squealed, and Reuben was never caught. But from that moment, something inside him wasn't the same.

Reuben was a good kid. He worked hard to make good grades in school. No wonder the school never suspected that it was he who tried to kill Pat. Neither did it surprise the administrators that someone was trying to kill Pat. He was a known gang member, and shootings, though not an everyday occurrence at West Mesa High, weren't unusual either.

The next time Reuben saw Pat, he told him, "Next time I won't miss. You and your gang members better back off."

Pat's gang had been trying to recruit Reuben to join with them the whole school year. When Reuben wouldn't go along with them, they began harassing him. Finally, he had enough and packed a gun with him to school.

One of the security guards noticed the pressure Reuben was under and guessed that he fired the shot. The guard knew Reuben was a good kid who just needed a break, so he told him he could use his address to get into a better school district where he could get away from the gang activities. Reuben transferred and graduated a few years later.

When Greg invited Reuben to come to church with him, he didn't know anything about his background. They were coaching a Little League team together, and the invitation was natural. Reuben didn't trust Greg because Greg was white and on staff at the church. But Reuben's wife was interested in going to church. So they did. And with time Reuben's life was transformed by the power of the gospel. It's a good thing because he was about to come face-to-face with the man he once tried to kill.

Reuben got a call to do some work at the Intel plant across town in Rio Rancho. As he was walking down the hall, he saw a face he hadn't seen in years, a face he could never forget. He saw Pat. Instead of the old hatred welling up inside him, Reuben felt conviction. "Can I talk to you a minute?" Reuben asked. "A lot has happened since we were kids in high school, and I wanted to tell you that not long ago, I became a Christian, and I want to ask you to forgive me for trying to kill you." Choked up, Pat responded. "Me too. Three weeks after you shot at me, I made a decision to follow Christ."

Once enemies. Now brothers.

In the weeks that followed, Reuben went to Pat's church to tell the story, and Pat went to Reuben's church—each testifying about the transforming power of the gospel. A gospel that changed their lives—and Jennifer's.

Skinhead

Sitting alone in a neatly arranged circle of cold metal chairs was a baldheaded, "extremely pregnant" white girl with the word *skin* tattooed on the back of her hand and a pack of cigarettes under her chair. It had been years, but Jennifer had attended this church when she was a little girl. She was back because she remembered the love her teachers showed her there, and increasingly she doubted that she was doing the right thing with her life. A man dressed in a blue double-breasted blazer, red tie, and tan pants, walked into the room, looked startled when he saw Jennifer, said hello, and darted back into the hallway. In a minute he returned, shared a moment of small talk, and then left the room again. Jennifer didn't say much that day, but she did listen.

The next Sunday she was back, this time more pregnant than the week before, wearing the same clothes, and with her pack of cigarettes under the chair. But this week she shared some of her story. It turns out she'd just returned from Idaho, where she was part of a neo-Nazi camp with the mission of procreating the Aryan race. After getting pregnant with her second child, she fled the camp and was hiding from the skinheads but was searching for peace. One evening someone came up to the pastor and said, "There's someone out front smoking. Will you go out there and tell her to stop?" Knowing exactly who it was, the pastor responded, "I'd rather have her here and smoke than not have her here at all." With time the power of God transformed Jennifer. She had the tattoo lasered off her hand, let her hair grow out, and eventually married a wonderful man—a Hispanic man who didn't speak English. She learned his language.

Jennifer didn't need to change her behavior or learn to become a more sociable skinhead; she needed a changed heart—something God specializes in. He did it for Jennifer, and he did it for Nikki too.

Completion

A Jew, reared attending temple, Nikki wanted absolutely nothing to do with church. She made that very clear to her friend Dana, who attended the Next Level Church in Denver, but Nikki agreed to attend "just once." The next Tuesday she was back. "I never stopped going," she said. "The energy that was present around me was all consuming and actually addictive!" Nikki wasn't a seeker; she wasn't seeking for God. The Scripture says, "There is no one righteous, not even one; there is no one who understands, no one who seeks God. All have turned away, they have together become worthless; there is no one who does good, not even one" (Rom. 3:10–12 NIV). She wasn't seeking God, but she said, "God was constantly seeking me out. I was asking for proof and finding it everywhere I looked."

Nikki had plenty of questions and went through a lot of confusion but realized that "in twenty-seven years of 'being' Jewish never was I 'being' with God, much less in any sort of relationship with him." On August 18, 1998, she realized that Jesus was the Messiah and her Savior. By God's grace she became a completed Jew. Her life radically changed.

"Today I experience God all around me," Nikki says, "because the hole in my heart is now full of ever-flowing love for God." And then there was David.

From Gay to Joyful

As a teenage boy, David noticed that he was more attracted to boys than girls, but not wanting to give in to those feelings, he did as the other boys did in his small Southern town—he dated girls. After graduating from college, he asked Brenda to marry him. But try as he might, he couldn't break from his obsession. After less than a year, he left Brenda to move to Vancouver, where he was free to act out his impulses. He never told Brenda why he left. He just left.

David lived the lifestyle. He went from one encounter to the next, until he settled down in a steady relationship and moved in with a man. Unlike some in the gay community, he was never careless in his sexual behavior. David always used "protection" and was regularly tested for HIV. But the condom didn't protect his soul.

One evening David's lover and several of his gay friends went to a nice restaurant to enjoy an evening out. Before long David was observing himself interact with the people at the table. He literally got sick to his stomach. The next Sunday he went to church. The people welcomed him, and he felt at home. He loved hearing the hymns from his childhood. The next week he went back and after two months made an appointment to speak to the pastor. His upper lip trembled as he reached in his shirt pocket to pull out a list of things he needed to talk about. He told the pastor that he was gay and was openly living the homo-sexual lifestyle, open to everyone, that is, except his wife and family back home. "I've come to despise what I've become," David said, "and want to change. But I want to know whether these feelings I have toward men will go away if I go back to my wife."

"No," the pastor said. "In fact, they will intensify." David stared silently at the pastor as he continued. "Satan will entice you even more if you try to walk away from this lifestyle." It got quiet in the room. The pastor continued, "The lifestyle you're living is unnatural. That's why AIDS is such a risk in the homosexual community. The body wasn't designed to do the things you've been doing with it.

"But not only is it unnatural," the pastor continued, "it is unbiblical. The Scripture calls it an abomination." David looked away. "Besides," the pastor said, "do you think it is fair to ask your wife to take you back after you've betrayed her trust the way you have? Instead of asking her to move out here and quit her job, you go back and tell her what you've become, beg her forgiveness, quit your job, and move back to where she is, and start dating her again."

They visited some more. After the hour for the appoint-ment passed, David folded up his list, thanked the pastor for his time, and stood up to leave. "Before you go," the pastor said, "let me answer a question you didn't ask. It will be worth it. It is the right thing to do." They prayed together. As David walked out the office door back to his car, the pas-tor thought to himself, *I'll never see him back here again.*

The pastor was wrong. The next Sunday, David was back, and the next and the next. About a month later he made another appointment with the pastor to update him. "I've moved out of my lover's house," David said, "and am working to reconcile things with my wife. I don't know if we'll get back together, but I feel good about what I'm doing. There's another question I want to ask you," he said. "I'm not sure I'm saved. Can you show me how to become a Christian?" "Now that's an easier question," the pastor said. "I'd love to."

That day David put his trust in Jesus. For a while it looked like he and his wife would reconcile, and she would fly in to see him baptized, but it never happened. Not yet at least. Two months later David entered the baptismal waters with his pastor. Not the same old David, he was transformed by the power of the gospel.

"Reaping the Whirlwind"

In the preface to their book *GenXers after God*, the authors point out that this is the first American generation to be raised in a secular culture—a generation born after America ceased to be a Christian nation. In their lifetime it has always been legal to have an abortion but illegal to have prayer in the public  schools. School officials are permitted to hand out condoms, but not Bibles. What happens when you sow the wind? "If you sow the wind," the saying goes, "you'll reap the whirlwind." Are we reaping what we've sown? Is the spiritual void causing a generation to act as if they are void of genuine spirituality?

Is a spiritual void the reason Eric Harris and Dylan Klebold took automatic weapons with them to school one day and wrought havoc on innocent people in a school cafeteria? The Next Level Church (TNLC) is doing something about the spiritual void in their city. They aren't paralyzed by the future and resigned to "reaping the whirlwind."

When security opens the doors, two thousand people rush into the low-lit room. Within minutes the room is filled to capacity, and the band starts playing. The music is loud—really loud. People stand, and Tuesday night worship at TNLC in Denver begins. No baby grand pianos, no plexiglas pulpits, no cheesy living room scenes, no floral arrangements. The atmosphere is more like a nightclub than a church building. Trevor Bron, founding pastor of TNLC, says that "people are created to worship, and they do it naturally. Some do it at rock concerts and others at sporting events." And some do it on Tuesday nights at TNLC.

Interactive Worship

"Did anybody bring any corn with them today?" Bron asked. "I did," a member of the congregation replied. As Bron walked into the crowd, the audience member pulled an ear of corn out of his sock and handed it to his pastor. Holding the corn in both hands, Bron asked, "Will you lend me an ear?" The crowd laughed. "Pastor humor," he added as he turned to walk back to the teaching platform, "is like normal humor, except not as funny." The crowd laughed again. Slowly Bron peeled back the shucks and taught about generosity. "All of this corn came from a single kernel, and each stalk has many ears of corn on it. If you want to harvest something, you first have to plant it." Building on this visual illustration, Bron taught a powerful lesson about generosity and the importance of tithing in the Christian life.

Bron often illustrated complex truths with simple objects. One week he used an artichoke (like truth—you have to pull it apart to enjoy the meat). Another week he took ten watches out of his pocket (everyone has time on their hands, but godly people use it wisely). And one week he used corn. Bron doesn't always use a prop. Sometimes he shows a movie clip, and other times he simply uses a strong story. "I don't feel the picture has to be 'physical' for the audience to 'see' it," Bron says. "That's why people read fiction." Bron makes no apologies that TNLC services last over ninety minutes or that his sermons are forty-five minutes long. He rejects the notion that GenXers have short attention spans. "Sporting events, movies, evenings out are all longer [than a TNLC service]," Bron says. "The key question is, Are they captivated? People will listen to a communicator if he is captivating."

Columbine

Becky was captivated. "If you are a friend or family member of Becky, will you please stand in her honor?" Several people stood and cheered. "Becky, do you know for certain that you've entered into a relationship with God and his Son Jesus Christ?" She said yes. The pastor continued: "In obedience to the command of our Lord and Savior Jesus Christ, I baptize you, my sister and my friend, in the name of the Father and the Son and the Holy Spirit."

As the pastor lifted Becky from the water, the auditorium erupted with applause. It was February 8, 2000, just another Tuesday night service at The Next Level Church in Denver. But not for Becky; for her it was a celebration of a new life— a night she and her friends will never forget. At the time Becky was a junior at Columbine High School. After the shooting, Becky started searching for something. That's when a friend invited her to attend church with her. At the Next Level Church, Becky found what she was looking for.

The Rise

After graduating from Colorado Christian University with a bachelor's degree in political science, Trevor Bron's university asked him to lead a Bible study for college students. Bron said no. He thought the last thing students at a Christian college were looking for was another Bible study, so he closed the door. A few weeks later the university called to see if he would lead a worship service. By the time Bron got back to them with a yes, they'd already decided not to go in that direction. The university closed the door. In August 1993 the university called again and asked if the Applewood Baptist Church, the church where Bron served as a staff member, would be willing to host a praise and worship service on Tuesday nights. This time, God opened the door.

On September 5, 1993 at 7:57 p.m., TNL (Tuesday NiteLife) began as a ministry of Applewood Baptist Church of Denver. Sixty people came. Within three years TNL was running over three hundred and was outgrowing the "ministry" status. At first it was an additional worship opportunity for college students, but by the third year many of the attenders didn't attend church anywhere else, and some of them weren't even in college. Bron's senior pastor rarely attended TNL. But one night he came. That evening Bron asked him, "How many of these people do you know?" Pastor Phil estimated that he recognized about 20 percent of them; he'd never seen the others. That night Bron realized that TNL was outgrowing the "ministry status" and was evolving into what he called "a church within a church."

Bron continued leading Applewood's Sunday morning singles' ministry and teaching on Tuesday nights, but he began feeling that he should put all his energy into TNL. At a John Maxwell conference in Denver, Bron sensed the Lord leading him to leave his staff position and do TNL full time, but before he spoke to his pastor about it, he wanted some confirmation. At home he sat down and opened his Bible. It fell open to Haggai, the heading on the page said, "A call to build the house of the Lord." Bron had his confirmation. Bron's senior pastor listened to everything Bron had to say when he talked to him about the possibility. "Before you do this," the pastor said, "pray about it for a year, then come and talk to me." Reluctantly Bron submitted to his pastor and prayed for an entire year and continued to minister in both capacities.

The church gave Bron a 12 percent raise that year. (The pastor was making it hard for him to leave.) For an entire year Bron prayed, "Lord, change my pastor's heart." Almost a year to the day, Bron's senior pastor came into his office, shut the door, and said, "I think it is time for you to start a church." Through the entire year of prayer, he hadn't talked to anyone about the possibility except his worship leader; now he had only a few months to put the pieces in place to launch the church. In August 1997, Applewood Baptist Church voted to sponsor TNLC, now The Next Level Church. On TNLC's fourth anniversary, Bron announced the decision to the fourteen hundred people in attendance. Within two months they'd outgrown the Applewood facilities and moved into other facilities, where they reached a high of thirty-three hundred average attendance four years later. For about 60 percent of the people, TNLC was their only church; the other 40 percent attended church elsewhere on Sunday and came to TNLC on Tuesday nights. For them TNLC was an additional opportunity to worship or a parachurch ministry where they directed some of their energy and time.

The Fall

Momentum was high, the spirit was contagious, and the future was bright. Then came April 1, 2001. On that date Trevor Bron resigned. The stated reason—"morally inappropriate behavior." Attendance went into a tailspin, plummeting 40 percent. Losing a dynamic leader is always a blow, but losing a founding pastor is a double blow. Most of the losses were from those who belonged to other churches and viewed TNLC as another worship opportunity or parachurch ministry. "There are a lot of attenders for whom this isn't necessarily their home church, but those, by and large, for whom this is their church haven't wavered through this process," says Executive Pastor Chad Leavitt. The community group ministry and Team TNL (Servant Leadership

Teams) hasn't really diminished. The core of the church is still strong.

New Beginnings

It's been a difficult time for the church. But the people have pulled together, ministered to one another, and are looking to the future. "I can't tell you what the future holds for TNLC, but I am very confident that it will continue to do great ministry," Leavitt says. For the first three months, staff members filled the pulpit doing tag-team teaching, but now Dave Terpstra has assumed the lead teacher position.

Terpstra attended TNLC for the last two years while completing his degree at Denver Seminary, where he was voted Preacher of the Year in 2001. He is a talented communicator who is familiar with the pulse and passion of TNLC. "Dave is very gifted and a sharp guy. He is not only able to communicate God's Word," Leavitt says, "but he does it in the context of where we've been as a church and where we are heading."

Definitely there have been changes, but the values are the same, and so is the passion to change the world. This trial has tested the strength of TNLC's core values, and it has come through with a new resolution to pursue their dream. "Life goes on, church goes on, God is still good, the sun still rises, and we still focus on the things that are important to us—community, authentic relationships, teaching, learning and studying God's Word, worshipping God, and giving back in passionate ministry," Leavitt says. "The dust is settling, and things are picking up. TNLC will go on and continue to do wonderful ministry in the areas God's called us to do." The future is bright; the potential is unlimited.

On November 6, 2001, Trevor Bron returned to TNLC to speak. He told the thirty-two hundred people who gathered to hear him confess that he was sorry for what he'd done, that he was wrong for doing it, and that he needs help, and then he asked his former congregation to forgive him. "I love this church," Bron said. "Please support it." The people responded by sending him thousands of cards of forgiveness. "It was a great night of extending grace and communicating the redemptive power of the gospel of Jesus Christ," says Mike Shepherd, the head of his restoration team. Bron's restoration team consists of four area pastors and one layman from TNLC. They meet weekly for two to three hours and work on character development. Bron is also seeing a counselor each week.

"We've seen him owning up to his stuff and doing what he's got to do to rebuild his character and to overcome his struggles. He is becoming a new man of humility and integrity," Shepherd says. "He has submitted to everything we've asked him to do."

The restoration team's primary goal is to help Bron restore his personal character and integrity. Secondarily, they want to restore him to the ministry. "We don't know when or where that will be, but we have no doubts that he has gifts and abilities that God can use again," Shepherd says. "We are committed to do whatever it takes to help him prepare for that timing, whenever God makes that obvious to us and to him."

Francis Xavier said, "Give me your small ambitions. Come, save the world." That's what The Next Level Church is doing. Nobody ever said changing the world would be easy or that they wouldn't face setbacks trying to do it. But TNLC members are resolved to be world changers. They have no small ambitions. They desire to "be the generation that God uses to change the world, maybe one last time."

You might say they are "reaping the whirlwind"—for Jesus Christ, that is.

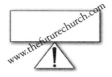

*C*onventional wisdom says that current culture will not tolerate duplicity and will immediately dismiss anyone who says
one thing and does another. They are suspicious of anything that
is slick, orchestrated, or too good to be true. What is the church's
response?

Fulcrum Point 4

Get Real

Robert Webber, professor of ministry at Northern Baptist
Theological Seminary in Lombard, Illinois, recently said,
"[Church] doesn't have to be excellent; it has to be real."[1]
While "Come experience fake Christianity" wouldn't make
a good slogan for anyone's church, and certainly no one
aspires to hypocrisy, churches in the past placed a stronger
emphasis on excellence than authenticity. Future Churches
place a higher value on being real than slick. They prefer
"raw Christianity" over "processed religion." No fairy-tale
endings. No happily-ever-afters. The emerging generations
demand straight talk and reality over platitudes and con-
trived, simplistic solutions. They strive for authentic community and encourage people to be real with themselves,
with God, and with others.

Because the reality of life includes pain and suffering, Future Churches acknowledge brokenness as a part of the human condition and encourage contrition for sin and absolute surrender to their sovereign God. Real authenticity isn't a crutch for sinfulness but a starting point for wholeness. It is being "poor in spirit"—spiritually bankrupt before a holy God and honest before his people.

"Seeking God's Heart"
Sandals Church, Riverside, California

"Matt, we've counted this week's offering, and it only came to $10. Is this all there is?"

The week before, Matt Brown quit his full-time teaching job to pour himself into the new church plant. Every indicator pointed toward going full-time. In just a year, the church grew to fifty, the people were enthusiastic, and his wife was supportive.

But now this. Had he made a huge mistake? Was he cut out for church planting? Could a congregation of young adults support a pastor? What now? "Yes," Matt said. "That's all." When he hung up the phone, he broke down and cried.

Slow Start

Sandals Church in Riverside, California, didn't happen after a long-term strategic study. In a sense it just sort of happened. In September 1997, Matt Brown, the founding pastor, resigned from his staff position as a youth minister at First Baptist Church of Fountain Valley and decided to start a church. His resignation grew out of frustration. The staff attended a John Maxwell Conference to discover how they could grow to a thousand by the year 2000. Brown sketched out a plan, but he and the church leadership couldn't come to terms on the new methodology. In the end the church didn't do anything. Brown was growing increasingly frustrated in his staff position and needed to make a change. "The truth is, they were equally frustrated with me," Brown says. "In seminary, church planting was like a frontier. It was cool, and a lot of people were doing it." But when it came right down to it, Brown didn't set out to start a church out of a sense of adventure, "Really, I had no other options," Brown said.

He chose Riverside because of all the good memories he had there. Riverside is the home of his alma mater, California Baptist University. Matt and his wife Tammy made a list of seventy-five people in the Riverside area whom they thought might form a core group to launch the church. Brown contacted Saddleback to see if they would sponsor the new church. Saddleback was willing to consider being the sponsoring church, but first they wanted to see a mission statement, a vision statement, and a purpose statement. Brown hadn't had time to write out any of these things; after all, he'd just left his staff position a week before. At the time Brown knew only two things: he wanted to start a church where people could be real with themselves, with God, and with others; and he wanted to call the church Sandals, based on Romans 10:13–15: For "'WHOEVER WILL CALL ON THE NAME OF THE LORD WILL BE SAVED.' How then will they call on Him in whom they have not believed? How will they believe in Him whom they have not heard? And how will they hear without a preacher? How will they preach unless they be sent? Just as it is written, 'HOW BEAU-TIFUL ARE THE FEET OF THOSE WHO BRING GOOD NEWS OF GOOD THINGS!'" To him the metaphor communicated a church with a servant's heart that was evangelistic; besides, it fit in nicely with the So Cal beach culture.

In the tradition of the purpose-driven™ church paradigm, Brown and his core group developed a Sandals acrostic with each letter standing for a word that describes the church's purpose. They even came up with twenty-one core values to present to Saddleback. But it wasn't working for Brown. Finally, he threw it all out. The purpose-driven model just didn't fit him. "Our purpose is to be very unpurpose driven—very relaxed," Brown says. "We're not going to move people around bases. That's very modern." Brown knew that postmoderns wouldn't go for that sort of thing. "People may start at three and move to two, then to four," Brown says. (Later Saddleback did help Sandals even though they didn't fit the purpose-driven church paradigm.)

Sandals doesn't claim to have found a universal formula to reach young adults, nor are they prepared to tell anyone else how they should do church. The pastors don't give the impression that they have "arrived" and are a bit nervous about anyone putting them in a box or on a pedestal. They are on a journey. "We're in process," Brown says. "We really don't know what we are doing. We just do what God wants us to do—like Abraham. God told Abraham to rise up and go to the land that he would show him." Sandals's effectiveness cannot be explained by personnel, location, design, or program but rather by their obedience. Like Abraham, Brown is obedient to get up and go, regardless of where his obedience takes him.

A Church on the Move

Sandals knows about moving; really, they are a nomadic church. They've met in eight different locations in four years. The church began in the Browns' home. When the group outgrew the living room, it moved to the Cabana Club, a multipurpose room in an apartment building. They've met in two different office complexes, a church basement, and the auditoriums of two different churches. Now they're settling in to their new home in a school gymnasium. When I caught up with them on May 6, 2001, they were in between meeting places. They'd signed a three-year contract to use the gymnasium at Cal Baptist, but it wasn't ready for occupancy yet. Their lease was up with the church where they were meeting. Graciously, the college let them set up seven hundred folding chairs on their lawn, and they held two outdoor services on the campus.

"It is easy to move a church of thirty people," says Nathan Brown, Matt's brother and the administrative pastor, "but almost impossible to move a church of a thousand." They looked at moving into a warehouse, but there were issues with parking, bathrooms, fire exits, and sprinkler systems. "It would cost half a million," Nathan Brown says. Just getting a "Conditional Use Permit" was going to cost around $40,000, and all that would get them was permission to move. It was possible to spend the money and have nothing to show for it. "The college already had a Conditional

Use Permit," Nathan Brown says. "It is worth gold to us." Now Sandals has a new place to call home. For a few years, anyway.

When he started the church, Brown was working full-time as a schoolteacher, attending seminary at the Southern California campus of Golden Gate Baptist Theological Seminary in Brea, and launching the church. "The first year was the most difficult year of my life," Brown says. At their first meeting in 1997, eight people came, and only three were from the original list of seventy-five prospects. Another week only four came. For a while, it didn't look as if the church would survive. The year was difficult, but it was also invaluable. "God made me more caring and compassionate," Brown explains. "He convicted me that I should preach passionately whether there are ten people or ten thousand [in attendance] because they deserve it."

"I envision the *Titanic* [when I preach]. I'm on the lifeboat and screaming for people to get in." At first they got in slowly. But then in September 1999, they flooded in. "That's when we brought Carlos Whittaker on to lead worship, and then we got momentum," Brown says. "People started getting saved. New people brought new people. Once we got momentum, it just continued."

Predominantly people in their early twenties were coming. But soon there was a smattering of people from all ages. Brown wasn't trying to start a church targeted to Gen Xers; he was just starting a church. "I have a passion to reach forty- and fifty-year-olds. They need Jesus," Brown says, "and we've got to reach them too." While some churches struggle to reach young adults, Sandals struggles not to look too much like a youth group. Students, grandparents, professionals, and academicians were all finding their way to Sandals. In a way Sandals was becoming the "in" church to attend. Because they met in the evenings, people who attended church elsewhere in the mornings would come to Sandals at night. Brown wasn't starting a parachurch organization and wouldn't settle for his church being a combination of a church and a parachurch, so one evening he told the audience, "Some of you are dating two brides. You need to pick a church!" The next week 250 people didn't come back. Brown doesn't regret what he said.

It isn't about numbers to the church. It is about being real. That's the vision at Sandals—being real. Not being trendy, large, influential, or famous. Sandals wants to be real—real with God, real with themselves, and real with others. This philosophy permeates everything they do and defines who they are.

Being real affects the messenger. Brown learned this lesson while still in college. In 1993 he spoke in chapel at Cal Baptist. At the end of the service, he gave an invitation, and 180 people responded. When he went to see his girlfriend (later his wife) at her dorm, she was crying. "What's the matter, babe?" Brown asked. "I'm just sad—sad that you're not like that all the time." The man she knew wasn't that man on the stage. Brown left her dorm purposing in his heart to become that man.

Beau Christian, a Corona police officer and member at Sandals, says, "I have seen our pastors do what they preach!" One evening one of the pastors called Christian to see if he could go with them to minister to a woman in his apartment building. "I saw not only that Sandals Church has taken the responsibility to protect themselves, as not to cause even the appearance of wrongdoing, but still to help those in need." They are real, on stage and off.

Being real affects the message. "The world says the answer is within," Brown says, "but we say the *problem* is within." People don't get sugar-coated pop psychology at Sandals. Brown shoots straight with the people. In the tradition of old-fashioned Bible preachers, Brown doesn't mince words with his audience. While clearly teaching what he believes, he challenges his audience to decide for themselves what they believe. "Every generation needs to grapple with what they believe, wrestle with it, and produce it," Brown says. "If we don't, we are as bad as the Jehovah's Witnesses." Some preachers try not to offend people. It's not that Brown tries to be offensive. But sometimes, to be real, a preacher has to risk offending people and tell them the truth.

Being real also affects the medium. "We've spent the last twenty years fighting over worship styles. This has stupefied our churches because we think it is a spiritual issue," Brown says. "It is the message, not the mode [of worship] that is important." Sandals's musical selections include hymns mixed with the newest music and some original pieces. Carlos Whittaker, service pastor, says, "I absolutely won't use music that is written just to sound good or that is theologically in error." Otherwise, it is fair game. The worship leaders don't perform. No plastered smiles or theatrical hand gestures. They just worship before the Lord and his people. They're real, and their worship is intense.

At other locations Sandals was able to use specialized lighting with their service but not anymore. Now they're coping with gym lights that take thirty minutes to come on and are either on or off, with no special controls. PowerPoint was out for a while until they could afford the equipment to "do it right." But it's not about technology and the latest teaching techniques. It is about being real.

There is an infectious simplicity to their worship services. "We're not really creative. Our church is simple," Brown says. "Songs, sermon, and go home. That's it! We don't want to waste people's time. A lot of 'stuff' can be distracting." The audience responds to Sandals's "cut to the chase" approach. In essence they are saying, "Give me what I need, and don't waste my time."

In many ways Sandals is cooking without a recipe. No plan, no strategy, no manuals, no organization. "It isn't about structure," Brown says. "We're on a journey, finding out what God wants us to do—seeking his heart."

Authenticity

The July 2003 cover of *Redbook* boasts a picture of Julia Roberts with the headline, "The Real Julia." I don't know if their coverage captured the real Julia or not, but the photograph certainly didn't. The picture on the cover was actually a composite featuring Julia's head and somebody else's body. Hearst, the magazine's publisher, issued an apology saying, "We acknowledge that we may have gone too far."[2]

May have? Hello? Saying something is "real" doesn't make it so. Actually, when it is, nobody has to say anything because everybody already knows. It is easy to talk about authenticity but much harder to be authentic.

Being "real" isn't as easy as it sounds. It reminds me of the struggle I have with wanting to be a humble person. Every time I feel that I've beaten down my ego and wrestled my pride into submission, I become proud of my humility and lose the battle with pride once again. One problem is that authenticity can become a "style" or a "mood" instead of a lifestyle. A friend of mine recently told me about a conference he attended where authenticity was a recurring theme among the speakers. When they spoke, they were deep, serious, and even a bit melancholy. There wasn't the customary veil between the stage and the audience. The speakers were quick to self-disclose their weaknesses and connect with the audience. There was a note of angst and contrition in the mood of the keynote addresses. Repeatedly, the speakers urged the listeners to be "real," to be themselves. But my friend noticed incongruence in the words of the speakers and their actions. In the hallways there was an energetic buzz and laughter. He noticed that many of the speakers had a great sense of humor offstage, yet he never noticed that same personality on the stage. They were too busy displaying their authenticity to be real.

As I listened to him tell the story, I immediately thought of the video clip I'd seen a few years ago of President Clinton, after a graveside service of a government employee. He was walking, laughing, and talking with a friend. But as soon as he saw the film crew out of the corner of his eye, he immediately teared up. Personally, I didn't have a problem with Clinton laughing because I know there can be joy in the midst of sorrow. But crying for the camera? Come on. That disgusts me.

Yet I've done it too. I want to be real, and I want the church I attend to be an authentic community of believers. But I also know that I will never be completely authentic, and neither will the church. Even when I open up and self-disclose, I don't tell everything. Besides, is it appropriate to tell every thought I have? The truth is, I am more like those conference speakers than I want to admit. There are times I'm preaching a message of joy when my heart is breaking, and there are times that I feign concern to conceal my apathy.

Kelly Williams, pastor of Vanguard Church in Colorado Springs, says, "The emphasis on realness is actually attempting not to be an intentional hypocrite." Maybe the blessing is in the sincere desire and the struggle. In the same way I'd rather be around prideful people who admit their frailty and work to be humble. I'd rather be around a hypocrite who tries to be real.

I was attending a ministers' conference at Hume Lake, California, last spring when one of my cabin mates told me about a meeting he attended with a group of church planters. They were gathering to talk about planting churches in a postmodern world. It wasn't a part of the printed program; it was just a group of guys that were ditching the planned stuff to sit in a circle and exchange notes.

He was jazzed about their first meeting. Their discussion that morning was on this very subject—authenticity.

I couldn't believe it. "I'd love to sit in on something like that," I said. "One of the chapters in the book I'm working on is on authenticity. Would you find out if I can sit in, ask a few questions, and record a session for me to listen to when I start writing the chapter?"

He asked the group if I could join them. What do you think their response was? They turned me down. Their reason for saying no was that they didn't want me to tape their answers to my questions. They didn't want to go on record. This was the first time someone wouldn't let me turn on the tape recorder during an interview. Most people understand that is insurance for accurate quotations.

I couldn't believe it. Not wanting to go on the record about authenticity? Come on. Authentic people don't care if someone quotes them. I came away thinking, *These guys may value authenticity, but they aren't authentic.* But then again, people who value authenticity are more likely not to be "intentional hypocrites." People who value it will lament their inconsistencies. I didn't know everybody in that group, but I did get to know three or four of the guys through the week, and they struck me as genuine, kind people. Chad Leavitt, executive pastor of The Next Level Church in Denver, says, "Authenticity has to do with being true to who you really are." Maybe saying no to me for whatever reason was their way of avoiding "intentional hypocrisy" and of "being true to who they really are."

Rounded Corners and Yellow Dots

Authenticity as a value coexists with our limitations and flaws. After McGwire hit seventy home runs in a single season in 1998, collectors scrambled to purchase his 1985 Topps rookie card. Con men were also scrambling—not to buy cards but to produce forgeries to sell to collectors. At $200 a card, con men were raking it in. The best of the fakes were hard to detect. Because they were screened from the original, they were a bit fuzzier, but only slightly. The real tip-off wasn't the imperfections of the fake but the perfections. For instance, the fake had sharp 90-degree angles on the borders; the originals were slightly rounded. The letters USA on the original have some random yellow dots surrounding them; the fake doesn't.[3] When I bought my McGwire rookie, I asked the dealer for a magnifying glass to see if I could spot the imperfections. When I saw them, I knew I was buying the real deal.

Being authentic means churches don't have to feign perfection and pretend to have all the answers or oversimplify complex issues. It is OK not to hide the yellow dots. It is OK not to have all the answers. Dieter Zander, a church planter in San Francisco, says, "If a sermon is too neat at the end, that discredits what you've talked about. There is a gut-level sense within [the listeners] that life is too easy to summarize in a thirty-minute message."

Jack Allen, pastor of Cottonwood Church in Albuquerque, never felt comfortable preaching the how-to sermons popularized in the 1980s by the contemporary church movement. "I always felt like I was trying to sell a used car," Allen said. "I don't say that to be ugly. It's just how I felt when I did it. It is perfectly fine to admit the realities of life. I struggle too when little girls get shot by some drive-by junkie, and I think it bothers God too." Today's listeners want the messages they hear to be realistic and the messenger to be real. "Authenticity is important," Allen says. "Postmoderns will openly mock and ridicule a teacher who has all the answers."

I like the way The Message paraphrases Matthew 7:15: "Be wary of false preachers who smile a lot, dripping with practiced sincerity. Chances are they are out to rip you off some way or other. Don't be impressed with charisma. Look for character."

Get the Picture?

Yes, the corners were rounded on McGwire's rookie card, and there were random yellow dots, but it was McGwire's picture on the card. Being real also means that McGwire's picture will be on his card. And for a believer, it means that one is growing in Christ. It is possible to fake imperfections in the name of being "one of the gang." People don't have to cuss or drink or make crude comments to prove they are human and can relate with sinners.

A few years ago I made a crude remark about a speaker to a person sitting next to me. It was the kind of comment that helped me bond with my buddies in the locker room when I was in junior high, and when I made it, I had that same kind of feeling of empowerment. You know, "I'm a preacher but I'm still a regular guy, and I can still relate to the common man." Mark Tabb, the person I made the remark to, took me aside later in the afternoon and said, "In the short time I've known you, I've come to know your heart, and I think of you as a godly man. But I've noticed sometimes you use language that I wouldn't expect to come from a man of God, and I think you should consider removing that language from your vocabulary. It doesn't become you." Initially I was defensive and downplayed the incident. But when I got by myself, God convicted me of my sin, and I've changed. Years have passed, and a couple thousand miles separate us, but Mark and I continue to be in frequent contact. He has become a close friend because he loved me enough to tell me the truth. And the truth was, I had some growing up to do.

Authenticity cannot become an excuse for not learning or growing. It is important to admit faults but not to learn to live with them in the name of authenticity. Ron Martoia, pastor of Westwinds in Jackson, Michigan, says, "The authenticity value rates very high—not wallowing in problems but being on the path to healing." Authenticity can never become an excuse to remain in a sinful pattern. Instead it will lead genuine believers to confess their sins.

Who, Me?

Does authenticity mean a person doesn't fail? Is it possible for a person ever to be totally pure? If we will all fail, what do authentic believers do when they fail? When authentic people fall, they admit their sins, confess them, and turn from them. Authenticity will eventually lead to confession.

King David was a man of contradictions. He was a hardworking man who was equally comfortable playing a musical instrument or fighting in a war. He was a tenderhearted poet with musical talents that could soothe the souls of his listeners. He was a "man after God's own heart"—a spiritual man. Yet David wasn't a softie. He was a warrior without peer. The people said of him, "Saul has killed his thousands, but David his ten thousands." David was a strong man, a leader of men, a man that anyone would feel safe walking beside. David was a spiritual man who penned many beautiful psalms that were sung in his day and read in ours. Yet David—a spiritual man—had a severe moral lapse.

It was the time of year when kings led their troops to war, but David was nowhere to be found. Instead of assuming his place in front of his troops, he stayed home. One night while walking around the palace roof, he spotted a beautiful woman taking a bath. Instead of turning his head and walking away, he stayed and watched. Later he sent for her and consummated his sin with her in the palace. She became pregnant. He tried to cover up his sin, even resorting to murder, but to no avail. His sin began when he was in the wrong place at the wrong time. He should have been at work where he belonged; he should have run when he was tempted.

But he didn't. David's sin became a defining moment in his life. It is too bad that he didn't finish his reign as strong as he started. He could defeat countless Philistines in battle but was overcome by the allure of a solitary woman.

When Nathan confronted David over his sin, he didn't cover it up. He brought it out in the open. He didn't say, "Hey, I'm in process, you've got to cut me some slack here. Besides, I may have gotten her pregnant and killed her husband, but I'm going to do what is right by her. I'm going to bring her into the palace." Mark Driscoll, pastor of Mars Hill Fellowship in Seattle, points out, "Being real and authentic when you are depraved is not noble. It may be who you are, but who you are may need to change." As an authentic believer, David confessed his sin and cried for mercy. Authenticity is never an excuse for sin. Instead it is a critical element of confession. Without it, people will never confess their sins because they will be too busy covering them up.

Authentic confession leads to spiritual brokenness. It will cause brokenness over sin, not pride for sin that wasn't committed. In his book *The Safest Place on Earth*, Larry Crabb tells the story of two men who experienced two different kinds of confession. Both were upset over a recent bout with sin: the first had kissed a woman who wasn't his wife; the other watched an X-rated movie in his hotel room while on a business trip. The first man was in tears when he confessed his sin to Crabb, but he was careful to state that the indiscretion went no further than a kiss. The conversation was half confession and half boasting—confession that he had kissed the girl, something he knew was wrong, but boasting that it didn't go any further. He was emotionally broken, but his pride kept him from being spiritually broken.

The second friend had a different attitude. He didn't minimize his sin by mentioning what he didn't do; instead, he expressed true contrition over his lasciviousness. He said, "I was thinking of no one but myself. I defiantly pressed the button and gave myself over to illegitimate pleasure for two hours. And yet God didn't throw me away. Something in me has changed. I know I'm capable of doing the same thing—or worse—again. But I feel a deepened desire to be with God, to draw close to him so that I'll have the power to do what I know I really want to do. And what I really want to do is to stay moral."[4]

Spiritual brokenness leads to a desire for righteousness and an acknowledgment of utter dependence upon God. People who are spiritually broken don't boast about sins they didn't commit. They are too busy for that kind of folly—too busy confessing the sins they did commit and pursuing righteousness.

The Real Deal

But even an imperfect, authentic person can be a person of character and integrity. And at some point, authenticity and integrity will intersect. Ray Kollbocker, pastor of Parkview Community Church in Glen Ellyn, Illinois, says, "Authenticity is the honest portrayal of ourselves before God and others as we seek to follow Jesus Christ." It may not denote perfection, but it does involve integrity. Integrity is everything. Former Senator Alan Simpson says, "If you have integrity, nothing else matters. If you don't have integrity, nothing else matters."[5]

Daniel was a man of integrity. He was so consistent that even his enemies could predict what he would do and used it to their advantage. Daniel 6:4 says, "Then the other administrators and princes began searching for some fault in the way Daniel was handling his affairs, but they couldn't find anything to criticize. He was faithful and honest and always responsible" (NLT). Daniel's enemies decided the only way they could accuse him was to set a trap. They convinced the king to sign a law that no one could pray to anyone but the king alone. Flattered, the king gladly signed the law without thinking how it would affect his friend Daniel.

Daniel's enemies knew he would break the law before he would pray to anyone other than the God of Israel. They spied on him, and sure enough, at the appointed hour for prayer, he faced Jerusalem and prayed, just as he did every day. They caught him "in the very act" of prayer and betrayed him to the king. They knew he would defy the king's law because Daniel was honestly living out his faith before God and others. Daniel didn't pray to show his integrity; he prayed because of his integrity. He was predictable because he was authentic. He had character and, in my view, was a true hero.

There is a difference between being a hero and being a mere celebrity. During the summer of 2003, the umpire caught Sammy Sosa using a corked bat in a game. It didn't take long for the baseball world to take sides over Sosa's indiscretion. Some say Sosa was trying to break out of his batting funk after being hit in the head by a pitch a few weeks before. Others took him at his word; he simply picked up the wrong bat as he was going to the plate—a bat that he said he used to put on a hitting show for the crowds during batting practice. Like most fans I wanted to believe Sammy because Sammy had become a celebrity and a hero—even to people who aren't baseball fans.

In an editorial for *USA Today*, Andrew Abrams offers some insight into the difference between celebrities and heroes. "Society is generally eager to forgive when its heroes occasionally stumble. However, consistent with heroic mythic, when the heroes falter because of character flaws, they must realize the error of their ways and seek forgiveness with sincere remorse. Often this realization and redemption, if anything, makes the hero even more heroic. Importantly, though, this redemption cannot come from a clutch home run or a game-saving acrobatic catch. The issue is not the physical prowess of the hero, but rather the individual's character, because talent without character creates celebrities, not heroes."[6]

Character does count. In the end it is the true measure of a man. You can measure the popularity of a man by the length of the shadow he casts on society, but the real value of the man is in the trueness of his heart. The talents God gives us are his gifts to us. What we do with them—the life of integrity we lead—is our gift back to him. No, I'm not talking about home runs, corked bats, denials, suspensions, or fines. I'm talking about living with integrity in the spotlight or in obscurity. We need people who don't use corked bats in games or in batting practice. We have enough celebrities. We need real heroes—men and women with character. Billy Graham says, "When wealth is lost, nothing is lost; when health is lost, something is lost; when character is lost, all is lost."[7] Psalm 26:1 contains this prayer for a person with character: "Judge me, O LORD; for I have walked in mine integrity: I have trusted also in the LORD; therefore I shall not slide" (KJV). Only people of character can invite the judgment of God in their lives and can say with confidence that they will not slide.

Having integrity and being authentic may be as simple as not using a false "preacher voice" when I speak—you know, the kind that makes "God" a three-syllable word. Or it may mean I'm not oozy-gooey nice all the time. Authenticity is not void of civility, but neither is it insincere. It certainly means I don't have to make myself the hero of every story I tell. But at times it may mean I have to publicly confess a sin and humbly receive discipline from the body.

Authenticity is important. I have no problem noticing when others are not being real. And I have a feeling they can notice it when I'm faking it too. If they don't, I know God does. And since I'm living my life before an audience of One, that's what matters the most. Pleasing the Father, living with integrity, having true character—being the real deal.

Brokenness

"Hello. . . . Yes, this is Mrs. Turner. . . . Yes, Officer, he's my husband. . . . You suspect him of what?"

With that phone call, Teri crossed the continental divide of her soul. She was numb. As she hung up the phone, life as she knew it ended. She would never be the same. Never! Twelve years prior the Turners had accepted their first ministry position together. At first Teri was a volunteer, but then, with time, she joined her husband's staff as a worship leader.

Being a ministry family was tough. Living in a fishbowl isn't easy for anyone, but compound it with the high expectations and isolation that accompany a church that places the pastor's family on a

ISSUES

pedestal, and it becomes unbearable. Teri and her husband dealt with the pressure differently. She poured her energy into her children and hobbies. He wandered deeper into his secret life—his sexual fixation with children.

Trauma Center

One Sunday Teri slipped into the service late and sat in the back row. She was enjoying the freedom of a day off and relished the thought of worshipping God without people evaluating the way she was dressed and how well she performed. She was doing fine, until about halfway through her husband's sermon entitled "The Church as a Trauma Center." Quietly she wept. Not because the sermon was moving or profound but because in her life the church and its pastor were creating trauma instead of treating it.

In 1994, she left her ministry position. Her husband resigned a year and a half later. They were unemployed, negotiating the purchase of an insurance agency when the phone rang that afternoon. With a plea bargain he got probation, and they worked at putting their lives back together and shielding the children from the fallout. Teri searched for a church home, but she couldn't find one. She didn't lose her faith or the consciousness that God was with her, but she couldn't feel God's presence anymore. The atmosphere of the churches she attended was "mandated happiness." By having services that were predominantly celebration, the churches were saying in effect, "It is not OK to be hurting." Teri didn't feel like singing and clapping, and the churches weren't providing an atmosphere for reflection or confession. "It was as if to go into those places you had to have your act together," Teri said, "or be dishonest enough to fake it." It was easier just to stay busy or to stay home.

In 1997, Teri found what she was searching for when she visited a new church started near her home. "The whole time I was at this service, I could tell right away there were a lot of people who didn't have a nice suburban life," Teri says. "The songs spoke to me. They weren't all in major keys. They were real and included the angst of everyday life. I went as a skeptic and came back as a participant." At this church there is time for silence. They have corporate confessions and readings that include the reality of pain and depravity. Teri emerged from the depths, breaking through despair that was suffocating her soul. When she reached the surface, she took a deep cleansing breath. For the first time in years, she worshipped.

Just when it looked like things were getting better, her husband violated probation. This time there would be no leniency. He was going to jail. Teri sat helplessly in the gallery as the district attorney put her children on the stand and grilled them. There was nothing she could do to protect them. But she wasn't alone. This time she had a church that stood with her—a church that is a trauma center, where it is OK to express brokenness and to find hope.

Brokenness isn't necessarily a bad thing. A farmer doesn't plant his crop in cement; rather, he chooses good soil, breaks it up, and then sows the seed. Unbroken soil does not produce abundant crops, but cultivated soil incubates life. A butterfly could never flutter in the spring air without breaking its cocoon, and neither could an eaglet emerge without breaking its shell.

Jesus could not feed the four thousand until he broke the bread (Mark 8:1–8). The sinful woman could not pour the costly perfume over Jesus until she broke the alabaster box (Luke 7:37). God could not reconcile himself to sinful man until he broke down the wall that separated him from us (Eph. 2:14). We could never know salvation without Jesus' broken body (1 Cor. 11:24).

In many ways we are not useful until we are broken. David wrote: "The sacrifice you want is a broken spirit. A broken and repentant heart, O God, you will not despise" (Ps. 51:17 NLT).

My Turn

A lesson I learned in 1995. I emerged through a foggy reality into a cold, unfamiliar room. I was hurting and struggling for breath. I tried to speak, but nothing came out. I lifted my right arm from the blanket and moved it around. Soon I felt the warmth of a stranger's hand. "You are OK, Mr. Wilson," she said. "The surgery went great. Your wife is anxious to see you."

Thirty minutes later they rolled me back to my room. Susan was there to greet me with a great big smile. "Was there any nerve damage?" I whispered. "What did the doctor say? Will my voice return?"

"He does not know yet. He will know more tomorrow."

The next day the anesthesiologist was the first doctor to come in the hospital room. "How are you doing, Mr. Wilson?"

"I can't talk!" I said in a raspy whisper.

"Do you mean it hurts to talk?"

"No," I screamed, "I can't talk!"

Shock appeared on her face. She began to fumble with her chart, said something about maybe it is temporary, and left the room without saying good-bye. I was getting nervous; I didn't like the look on her face. She knows something! What happened in that operating room? We would know in a little while; the surgeon said he would be there before noon. We waited for the surgeon, but he did not come. Lunch came, but the surgeon didn't. Dinner came, but the surgeon didn't. Finally, we called his office. I began thinking the worst. Something is wrong, and he is afraid to face me! That's why he's late.

Finally the surgeon arrived. I saw the disappointment on his face when I whispered, "Hi Doctor." Sitting on the side of my hospital bed, the doctor tried to explain why I couldn't speak above a whisper. During the surgery to remove my cancerous thyroid, he tapped on the recurrent laryngeal nerve, thinking it was fatty tissue. The assistant surgeon assured the doctor it was not the nerve and advised him to cut it. Twice he asked for an instrument to sever the structure, but when he tried, his hand froze. But because he tapped on the nerve, it no longer transmitted the signal from the brain to the vocal chord, leaving my right vocal chord paralyzed.

"But doctor, I'm a preacher. What do I do without a voice?" I stared into my doctor's eyes. "Will my voice come back?"

He blinked and looked away. "I don't know. Maybe, since I didn't cut the nerve, normal function could return in a few months. Or it could be permanent."

Suddenly my theology and this bizarre reality rammed together, full force, in a head-on collision. In that moment I had more questions than answers. *Will I ever preach again? How will I earn a living? What about my family? Where are you, God?*

That night I lay in bed as a thick silence surrounded me. "God, I'm over here," I prayed. "Are you watching? Why are you doing this to me?"

Don't Pray for Me Anymore!

In the beginning people's prayers touched me. One evening a little six-year-old girl prayed, "Jesus, please give preacher back his voice so we can listen to him preach again." I knew that God would answer the prayers of this little angel. But as time was running out, I resented people's prayers. They were constant reminders to me that God wasn't doing anything to help me. Everyone tried to put on a strong front for me. Their prayers were always upbeat, dripping with faith. I often felt like I was the only one in the room that was facing the reality that I might never talk again.

One staff meeting I upbraided our ministry staff for spending so much time praying for me. "Maybe someone would get saved around here if you guys would spend some time praying for the lost instead of me!" No one said anything. They were deer in my headlights.

The week before my second surgery, we dropped the kids off at my parents' home and went to a church conference center. I thought it would help if I could hide in a corner and escape my problems. No such luck. The conference leader was an interactive, sit-in-a-circle-and-talk-about-your-feelings kind of guy. He broke us into small groups to talk about our churches. My turn came. I whispered, "I'm pastor of . . . ." We finished early, so the guy next to me asked me what was wrong with my voice. I could see his heart through his eyes; he was a sincere man, so I told him.

The speaker began to call the groups back to attention. My new friend turned into my worst enemy when he interrupted the speaker to tell him about my situation and asked him to lead in prayer for me. I didn't want interaction, pity, attention, or prayers. I just wanted to be silent before God and his people. That was the first day of a weeklong conference. I never returned.

In my bleakest days I thought God was punishing me for something and that my voice would never return. "God will heal you," my mother said. "He wouldn't call you to preach without supplying you a voice."

"Yeah, Mom, He will heal me, just like he healed Lori." What was I saying? My little sister had died less than a month earlier from lupus. How could I be so insensitive to my mother that I would say something like that?

"All I know, Mom, is I'd rather die than not be able to preach. What good is a preacher without a voice?" The lines of grief were blurring. I was starting to think that Lori's fate was better than mine. In my own self-pity I was hurting my mom, who was trying to minister to me.

Attendance began to drop. People stopped joining the church, and we fell below the budget. I began to fear the worst. Because of my obvious depression, one family in the church accused me of "being unspiritual" and told me they were leaving. Another family was mad because I did not have morning devotionals at a church retreat. These families delivered a one-two punch to my midsection within days of each other. I felt powerless against my "unspiritual" depression and helpless that I was unable to speak loud enough to bring a simple devotional.

But most of all I was frustrated that I couldn't say what I was thinking. *This could be it. I could be losing my ministry.* The guest preachers preached sermons about dealing with adversity and having faith to overcome life's problems. They were good sermons—the kind of sermons I'd preached a million times. But they didn't resonate with my soul. I'd never really been broken before—not like this. I came to see people's "faith talk" as a defense mechanism to keep them from entering into my pain instead of a spiritual virtue to give me hope.

I'd stand among a crowd at church and feel very alone. I never cried—not when the doctor told me it was cancer or even when the surgeon said I might never talk again. I never cried, that is, until I crashed at the bottom one Sunday morning. We opened the service singing, "I Love You, Lord." The atmosphere was upbeat. There was a good crowd in attendance, and we had a fine guest speaker on the platform. I stood next to him and began mouthing the words to the song, "I love you, Lord, and I lift my v . . . ." There it was, that word, hanging in the air. I began to weep. Quietly I sobbed, trying not to disrupt the service. I was painfully aware that I couldn't make others aware of my pain. It wasn't OK. And that made it worse.

I've always struggled with anger. But for the first time in my life, my anger was white hot—so hot it was inexpressible. How could God call me to preach and take away my voice to do it with? Why did he make me go to college and seminary for ten years and three degrees if I couldn't use what I learned there? Anger really isn't the word. I was livid!

Then I looked at my wife and children and wondered how I could support them. I didn't savor the notion of cashing a disability check every month and trying to stretch it for the rest of my life. Believe me, these were hard days. I prayed for God to deliver me until I couldn't pray anymore. For almost a year I whispered or croaked, but I didn't talk. Then, after a third surgery, God worked his miracle and healed me.

Putting the Pieces Back Together

"Going once, going twice, sold for $7,000!" The auctioneer's gavel hit the table, and Rita Coors was elated. She'd just purchased a porcelain mask, hand painted by John Denver. She couldn't wait to hold it in her hands. As the auctioneer at the 1997 Charity Celebrity Ball for Hospice of Metropolitan Denver handed her the mask, it slipped through her fingers and shattered into a million pieces on the floor.

She didn't abandon the shattered art; instead she placed the broken pieces around a collection of John Denver photographs. She made something beautiful out of the accident. Now she not only had a souvenir from a celebrity but a story to tell too.[8]

When life slips through our fingers and shatters at our feet, the best thing we can do is pick up the pieces, make something beautiful out of it, and then be willing to share the story with others who've been shattered too. There is healing in telling our story. There is healing in hearing someone else's story too.

When doctors removed the ulcer next to Bob Sorge's larynx, they permanently damaged his throat, leaving him with a remnant of a voice that hurts if he tries to "whisper" more than an hour a day. A terrible tragedy for anyone, but the suffering was multiplied for Sorge. Rev. Bob Sorge, that is. Like me, Sorge lost his voice to a medical procedure, but unlike me, he hasn't gotten his voice back. "God is to be wrestled with," Sorge says. "He has unfolded purpose to me. He's transformed the way I think, feel, everything about me. The crucible of suffering causes you to be desperate for God and to press into him."[9] Reading Sorge say his suffering makes him "desperate for God" ministers to me. And when I read that he wants to "press into him," I feel like a small child again, safe and secure in my Father's arms. And I want to "press into God" too. It is OK to be vulnerable before the Lord and his church. It is OK to be broken.

Today, if God said to me, "I'll give you that year back. You can go back to a cancer-free state, you can relive the year with your voice and without cancer, but you'll never know the loyalty you experienced from a church that stood beside you, or the love that you came to know from your bride who lived her wedding vows, 'in sickness and in health' before you, and you will never know that your brokenness is covered with my grace," I'd say, "No thank you. I'll keep the cancer."

Out of the brokenness I found peace. In the silence I heard God. I feel secure "pressed into him." Today I speak as freely about my doubts as I do my faith and about my pain as I do my joy because God is in both extremes. The one gives context for the other. And in both, God is glorified.

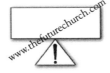

Conventional wisdom says that people no longer believe in absolute truth and are suspicious of experts, institutions, and anyone who makes exclusive claims. What is the church's response?

Fulcrum Point 5

Get Truthful

According to pollster George Barna, the number of Americans who agree that there are "absolute moral truths that fit into any circumstance" declined from four in ten to two in ten after the terrorists attacked the Pentagon and the World Trade Center on September 11, 2001.[1] In another poll the Barna Research group found that "only 9 percent of born again teens believe in moral absolutes and just 4 percent of the nonborn again teens believe that there are moral absolutes."[2] I'm not sure what explains the sharp increase in relativistic moral thinking, but my best guess is that the display of such intense evil rocked more than the foundations of our buildings; it also rocked our moral and ethical foundations. Left with more questions than answers, some people lost their bearings and took a step closer to moral chaos. Whatever the reason for the decline, it is a fact of twenty-first-century life that the vast majority of people do not believe in absolute truth.

In addition to the changing way people view truth, the deconstructionism and decentralization of information in postmodernity has changed the way people view experts. Experts are suspect at best and dismissed as egotistical blowhards at worst. So how does the church proclaim the absolute claims of the Bible in a relativistic age that is suspicious of authority figures? Future Churches aren't hedging their beliefs in the least; they are boldly proclaiming truth as they see it, but they do it without a condescending tone or without taking the expert vantage point. Instead, they allow their listeners to make up their own minds about what to believe, without compromising their own beliefs.

"A Hill Worth Dying On"
Vanguard Church, Colorado Springs, Colorado

After a handful of people left, Kelly stood in an empty room staring at the snowflakes as they floated from the  night sky to the ground. He prayed. "God, planting a church is hard enough without you making it snow every Tuesday!" All his life, Kelly had romanticized about starting a church, but no one ever told him it would be like this. He worked hard to meet people, develop relationships, and invite them to attend an "X-Group," a gathering for people to discuss their spiritual questions. He expected some opposition, but sometimes it seemed that even God was working against him.

Emotionally, he began to feel like raw meat going through a grinder. He was spent.

Some weeks only two or three showed up. Some weeks a dozen came. One week nobody came. That was the night Kelly faced his worst fear—the fear of being a failure. *I can't take it anymore*, Kelly thought. The more he thought about it, quitting became more appealing. Kelly began to work out the details of what he'd tell his supporters, his family, and his wife. It looked as if he couldn't rescue his dream, but at least he could save face.

The Dream

In June 1996, Kelly and Tosha Williams were holed up in a hotel room in New Orleans, looking their future straight in the eyes. And as they did, they had more questions than answers. All they knew for sure was that they wanted to follow God's will for their lives, but what was his will? With nothing but a pen and a pad of Post-It notes, they listed their questions. Should we start a church? Where should that church be? What denomination? Soon their future and the future of thousands of souls they might reach were defined by questions that filled a dozen or so yellow Post-It notes.

Williams grew up on a dairy farm in Kentucky in the home of a bivocational pastor who often dreamed of starting a church but never did. Perhaps it was his father's unfulfilled dream that drove Williams to start a church. Or maybe the dream was his. Kelly met Tosha while attending Liberty University in Lynchburg, Virginia. When they talked about their future, church planting always came up.

It was as if it was their destiny, but when? Would it be at the beginning of their ministry, or after they got more education and experience under their belts?

There was always the dream, but maybe the reason Williams became a church planter when he did was simply that he didn't have any other options. For a while it looked as though Williams would get his chance to complete a Ph.D. at Oxford. Williams's plan was to further his education at the prestigious university and then come back to the States to start a church. The professor he wanted to study under accepted his proposal, but the admissions committee turned him down. That was plan A, but he still had plan B to fall back on.

While attending Dallas Theological Seminary, Williams was the youth pastor at a Southern Baptist church in nearby Grand Prairie. When the church lost their senior pastor, the pastor search committee approached Williams to see if they could consider him for their next pastor. *Maybe that's why Oxford fell through,* Williams thought. *God wants me to get some pastoral experience before I start a church.* When that door slammed shut, Williams's options were limited.

What else could he do? After hearing Robert Reccord, president of the North American Mission Board of the Southern Baptist Convention, preach a stirring message on the passion to reach the lost, Williams decided to plant a church and to stay with the denomination of his youth, the Southern Baptists. But where could he start a church that was "real"? Not a cookie-cutter church or a church where people could be comfortable with their assumptions and hypocrisies. He wasn't necessarily impressed with tradition or innovation; he just wanted his church to be a place where people could be real.

After walking past several closed doors, Kelly and Tosha found one wide open in Colorado Springs. It had a large Gen-X population, his initial target group, but did Colorado Springs need another church? After spending a week in the city in July 1996, Kelly and Tosha packed their belongings in a U-haul truck and moved to Colorado Springs to plant a church.

Great Beginnings

In the beginning it looked as if all the pieces would fall into place. On the trip Williams prayed that he would meet some lost people he could witness to, preferably a man who could help him unload the moving van. Williams found a spot to park in front of his apartment building, got out of the moving van, and watched God answer his prayer.

"Moving in?" a man asked as he walked toward Williams.

"Yeah," Williams said. "We just pulled into town."

"Need any help unloading the van?"

"Steve" had just gotten out of the Navy and was considering moving to Colorado Springs. He helped Williams move in. It was the start of a new friendship, a reciprocal relationship of one person helping another. Steve helped Kelly move in, and for the last five years Kelly and Tosha have loved Steve and his family into a real relationship with Jesus Christ.

A couple of days later, the super came to the apartment to fix a problem with the pipes. She had an androgynous name, looked like a man, and worked in a profession that is predominantly male, so it is understandable that Kelly thought she was a man. During their conversation she talked about just losing her mother to cancer, and Kelly talked about his mother being killed by a drunk driver.

They connected. "Would you like to have dinner with me and my wife?" Kelly asked. "Sure," she replied. "Do you mind if I bring my friend?" Little did Kelly know at the time that she would bring her lesbian lover. In time they both came to faith in Christ, and Williams baptized them. One of them drifted back into the lifestyle, but the other became a missionary in Japan teaching English as a second language.

Another day a local news anchor knocked on the Williams's door. She'd heard about the new church start, and she was looking for some spiritual guidance. Kelly listened to her pour out her heart. When it was his turn to speak, he told her that Jesus, who claimed to be God, wanted to have a personal relationship with her. She'd never heard that Jesus claimed to be God; she just thought Christians made that up. Later she did a story on the church, and Williams was able to get the word out about Vanguard to her viewing audience. At the beginning it looked as though they were blessed and that the start would be almost effortless, but not now. Now it seemed that they were cursed. *How am I going to explain this to Tosha,* Kelly thought. *She's always believed in me—and the dream.*

Kelly opened his Bible to the day's devotional passage— John 10, the discourse on the Good Shepherd that lays down his life for his sheep. As he read, Kelly heard God's voice: "I know you are willing to be a success for me, but are you willing to be a failure for me? Are you willing to lay down your life for these sheep?" His open Bible opened his heart.

"Yes Lord, yes!" Williams prayed. "I'll lay down my life for these sheep. If it is your will, this is the hill I'll die on. I'll fight to the bitter end."

With that prayer Vanguard was born. *Oxford Dictionary* defines *vanguard* as "the foremost part of an army or fleet advancing or ready to do so." The militaristic name resonates with the Colorado Springs military community. There are four military bases in Colorado Springs, including the Air Force Academy. But it has a deeper meaning than that. Williams desired to pastor a "front lines" church, a church that would take the hits to live out their mission: "Loving people into a real relationship with Jesus Christ." And, if necessary, he was willing to lay down his life in the process.

"I like how the church growth books will say at this point in the story, 'And after that prayer thousands showed up,'" Williams says. "But months passed and nothing changed." Instead of making plans of how to exit gracefully, Kelly started making plans on what he would do when his start-up resources ran out. Finally the twelve-member core group decided it was time to take the church public and have their first service. To get the word out, Williams went to a secular radio station to buy ad time. After discussing options, the advertising salesman drew up a contract for $15,000 for one year's advertising. Five thousand dollars of the plan was for the first two weeks. Williams stared at the paper, took a deep breath, and reached for his pen. Two weeks later they held their first R-rated service (R stands for "real"), and seventy-five people came. They never really dropped below that figure.

Multiplex Worship

Today Vanguard Church holds three weekend services in a multiplex movie theater that the church renovated to house its expanding ministry. Church in a movie theater has its advantages. For one, the logistics are great for showing movie clips in the sermon. Actually, it is larger than life. And the sound is awesome. But the primary advantage is the sloped floor. In a world where information is decentralized and people are suspicious of experts, the ambiance created by the sloped floor facilitates Williams's relational preaching style. "I'm not focused on a transference of information or a process of change," Williams says. "I'm focused on an experience of relationship. If that relationship can take place, then the other things can take place." It is a subtle yet important distinction. "In the past, a modernistic thinker would say, 'God created you, and if you'll look at the world, you will see it, and you'll have to come to terms that God made you,'" Williams says. "I may say, 'I believe God created you. Now you may not believe that, that's a decision you have to make. But for me, I've made that decision.'"

It took a lot of trust and personal security for Williams to move from an informational to a relational preaching style—trust in his audience that they are intelligent and trust in God that he will speak to the people. "It is trusting that there is a power within people that will cause them to make a commitment," Williams says. But it also took personal security—to be secure enough in what he believes that he can feel good about what he believes, even if everybody in the audience doesn't agree with him. And sometimes people don't agree with Williams's message—like the Sunday seventeen people walked out in the middle of his sermon.

Vanguard often uses secular images and icons to make spiritual points. The special music before the sermon is more likely to come from the Beatles than the Gaithers. Williams uses the secular to help people make a spiritual connection. And for most people, it works. "I turn on the secular radio, and I hear these songs," one worshipper told Williams. "But I come into the service and see how you attach them to the Bible and the context of our lives, and you show what they are crying out for with these songs. And now when I hear them, I think of God." But then there are those who are offended by the use of secular icons in a sacred place. Sometimes being real can be raw, and it rubs some people the wrong way. The week seventeen people walked out of the service, Williams showed the video clip of a scantily clad Britney Spears performing with Aerosmith during the 2001 Super Bowl halftime show.

Before showing the video, he read several clips from news sources about Spears, including an interview with *Teen People* published in February 2000, in which she said, "I'm a Christian. I go to church." Williams also read the lyrics to the song she was singing—a song about oral sex. Then he showed the video. After showing the video, Williams said, "Don't call me and complain about me showing this video in church if you watched it at home and it didn't offend you there. But if you didn't see it at home, and you want to know why I showed it here, give me a call, and I'll talk to you about it."

Using raw reality like the Spears clip in worship services troubles the hypocrisy in people's lives—"the hypocrisy that says, 'Don't make me look at the real me.'" Williams says. "Let me live in my facade and my assumptions. Don't let me think about what I really need to change."

"We are often asked, 'Should we be doing this in church?'" Williams says, "when what they should be asking is, 'Should we be doing this at all?'" Is it appropriate to show that kind of video clip in a worship service? Probably not. But that's not the question Vanguard asks. They would rather ask, "Is it profitable for the kingdom's sake?"

"Appropriateness is about social customs; profitability creates a sense of God's presence." Williams says. "It makes you ask, 'Would this be profitable to what God is trying to accomplish in this context?'" Their focus is steadfast. They are loving people into a real relationship with Jesus Christ. "That's all that matters," Williams says. Vanguard's services may not always be appropriate to people who grew up in church, but one thing you can count on: they will never promote intentional hypocrisy—they are real. "I'm tired of being in a Christian subculture that acts out religion. I don't want to pretend I'm fighting a war on Sunday and going home during the rest of the week and doing nothing about it," Williams says. "I want to be a part of a real battle of good and evil. I either want to win the battle or lose it, but I want to be in the battle."

And he and the people of Vanguard have found a hill to fight that battle of good against evil—a hill worth dying on.

"In Your Face" Compassion

Pastor Kim is active in sharing his faith, leading twenty-five of his peers to Christ over the past year. He didn't lead twenty-five pastors to the Lord; he led twenty-five prisoners to the Lord. Pastor Kim is serving a three-and-a-half-year prison sentence for charges leveled against him by the Uzbekistan government.[3] Even

though he suffers severe beatings for sharing his faith, he continues to bring the light of Jesus to the darkness of the prison. Like the apostles of old, Kim and other evangelistic Christians cannot stop sharing their faith. "We cannot stop speaking what we have seen and heard" (Acts 4:20 NASB).

Pastor Kim is showing unusual compassion: even under the threat and reality of beatings, he continues to share his faith. Why? Because it does matter what people believe, and telling them the truth is the compassionate thing to do.

It is easy to go with the flow and tell people what they want to hear. It takes an unusual compassion to go against popular culture and be a truth-teller.

Mark Driscoll, pastor of Mars Hill Fellowship in Seattle, is a truth-teller. He approaches his life and his ministry with a zest for pursuing and proclaiming the truth. His approach is direct, and his motivation is transparent love—love for Christ and his people.

Sin and Grace in Your Face

The Mars Hill liturgy is simple: sin and grace. The service opens with a couple of introspective songs that remind the people of their sinfulness and evoke confession. Then and only then does the light of the gospel shine with grace. Pastor Mark Driscoll, the self-described "disenfranchised, punk-rock fundamentalist," says, "Culture has no center. It is fragmented. The only thing that binds people together is utter depravity and selfishness. Our message is sin and grace. It isn't sexy or cutting-edge, but it is biblical." After the people are prepared to hear the gospel by reflecting on their own sinfulness, Driscoll begins his sixty-minute exposition of the Bible—so much for the short attention span of Generation X. "They tell you church is supposed to go an hour with only twenty minutes of preaching," Driscoll says, "but I preach an hour, hour and a half." At Mars Hill, the preaching of the Word is the focal point of the service.

Unlike other Future Churches, Mars Hill doesn't use the arts in the worship services. In the beginning they used painting and dance but not now because, in Driscoll's estimation, "most of it flopped." Today they stick to what they do well: preaching and music. "I don't do art. I don't do [video] clips. I just preach the Bible," Driscoll says. "I tell people they are wicked and God loves them and Jesus is their only hope." Driscoll's sermons are verse-by-verse expositions. He preaches without notes or even a game plan; he simply studies the passage of Scripture and preaches extemporaneously. He preaches "on the fly"; the structure isn't planned. It is either intuitive or instinctive. Driscoll interjects stories and illustrations into the exposition as they come to mind, but he doesn't plan them out in advance.

A large part of his preparation is the time he spends alone with God in prayer and in solitude. It is in the solitude that the studying and reading he's done steeps like a cup of tea. "My hope is to be guided by the Spirit," Driscoll says, "but I'm a sinner, and sometimes I preach my own agenda. The key [to being guided by the Spirit instead of preaching my own agenda] is in spending time in solitude and prayer." Because his messages are extemporaneous, Mars Hill doesn't use PowerPoint during the message. Driscoll doesn't apologize for the simplicity of his services. "It isn't about being cool or hip; it is about me standing up and giving the people a word from God so they will be refocused toward a Godward orientation and off themselves so God can do something in and through them for his glory, not their own."

The messages include heavy biblical content with strong ethical application. His preaching style is in sharp contrast to felt-needs preaching, popular in the contemporary church. Felt-needs preaching, according to Driscoll, is void of "theological rigor" and uses a "man-centered" theology and hermeneutic. "Preaching becomes principles for empowerment, principles for success and victorious Christian living. Most of the preaching is about people, not about God."

Driscoll doesn't begin with a "felt need" and mention the Bible in passing; he goes straight to the Bible to address his audience's greatest need—their sinfulness. "We don't start with Jung, Freud, or Maslow; we start with the Bible.

In a world with darkness and an enemy, we need shepherds, not hand-holders, but those who will fend off wolves. We need men with theological rigor, not just people who will flow with culture."

When he preaches, Driscoll pulls no punches. His sermons are straight to the point. They aren't cute, clever, or gentle. And they certainly don't try to appease popular culture. They are "in your face" biblical—not street preacher rude but direct, nonetheless. "The gospel demands that I be countercultural," Driscoll says. "Not culturally relevant but culturally offensive, not in a way that repels people but one that actually attracts people because it is so 'other.' We've lost a sense of holiness—that God is different and God's people are to be different. People have plenty of psychologists and therapists; what they need are preachers who will preach the word."

At the conclusion of the message, there is a protracted time of silence so people can listen to God, followed by communion. Eight pairs of elders stand at the front of the auditorium, one elder holding a broken loaf of bread, the other holding two large cups of juice. One at a time people take a piece from the loaf, dip it into the cup, and return to their seats. The music begins, but this time it has a note of celebration to it. After refocusing on Christ with communion, the congregation is ready to celebrate the fruit of the gospel.

Leveraging Culture

When I worshipped with the people of Mars Hill, they were settling into their seventh location. The Ballard location served as a base of operation for the church's ministries, but it wasn't the only place they gathered. They also met on Sunday evenings in the seedy U-District of Seattle in an old two-hundred-seat theater purchased by one of the church's elders, Lief Moi, a local radio host. During the week the Paradox Theater encourages the musical creativity of the "city with ten thousand bands" by hosting local, national, and international shows that play to over one thousand people a week. The church has a recording studio in the theater that is filled with business from non-Christian bands. Many of the musicians have come to Christ and are now active in the music ministry of the church, continuing to play in venues throughout Seattle and serving as missionaries to the music culture. For eight years Mars Hill broadcast the nationally syndicated radio show *Street Talk* on Christian radio in eight markets. Airing on Saturday nights from nine to midnight, the program included the music of live bands and dialogue with youth and young adults about the gospel.

In March 2003, the church moved into their new forty-thousand-square-foot church home and consolidated their ministries into the central location. The Paradox ministry continues in an area of the new location. They continue to do indy rock and punk shows for non-Christian kids in a venue that seats four hundred and in the main room that seats fifteen hundred.

Mars Hill Fellowship isn't adapting to culture; it is leveraging it to proclaim the gospel. Their name indicates that. In Acts 17, the apostle Paul stood on Mars Hill and spoke to an assembly of the Areopagus to proclaim the gospel. During his witness he referred to their beliefs, poets, and sculptures to illustrate the gospel truth. Paul wasn't culturally relevant, but he used the culture to proclaim the gospel. Driscoll advises church leaders, "Love God and do what fits in your area; think like a missionary, and put the gospel wherever you happen to be." That's exactly what he is doing—loving God, thinking like a missionary, and doing what fits in his area. Because Seattle's culture is driven by music, Mars Hill Fellowship is using that vehicle to proclaim the gospel.

Their service moves with a distinct urban beat—a coffee-sipping rhythm. It is relaxed on the surface, but beneath there is a stirring. The music evokes angst and surfaces inner pain; it is dark, but it is also meaningful. There is a note of reflection in the music. Definitely it isn't feel-good, canned, commercial stuff; instead it has an underground, garage-band feel to it—more like something you would hear out of England than Nashville.

Mars Hill is serious about their music. The church's composers have set over one hundred hymns—prayers of the early church fathers, creeds of the church, and the fresh words of their own poets—to music for their five bands. They have always composed their own music, even in the beginning. The official launch of the church came in the fall of 1996, with a first service attendance of around two hundred that soon leveled off to one hundred. That's when the church began its public meetings, but in many ways the church began in Driscoll's heart many years before, even before he was a Christian.

God's Calling

For a high school graduation present, Grace, his girl-friend, gave him a New Testament. He read the book through in just over a week. God was working in his life. One evening a buddy asked him what he was planning to do as a career. Driscoll replied, "I think God is going to make me a Christian and send me out to plant churches like the apostle Paul." Not sure if Driscoll was mocking him, his Christian friend laughed. Within a month Driscoll surrendered to the gospel, and within six months he surrendered to God's call in his life. Kneeling by an Idaho river on a retreat, he sensed God saying to him, "I have called you out from among many to lead men." After graduating from college, Mark and Grace—now married—moved to Seattle to begin planting churches. They didn't have jobs or a place to live, but they had something more concrete than those things—they had God's call upon their lives.

For a while Driscoll served on staff of a church working with college students, learning all he could about church leadership. Slowly he began to meet people and form a core group to begin praying about planting a church to reach the emerging generations with a postmodern worldview in one of the most unchurched cities in the United States—Seattle. But today the vision is larger than a single city. To date they've planted over one hundred churches in eight countries and are growing at a rapid clip. They have more qualified church planters than they can fund.

Driscoll wants to plant a thousand churches and is working with the Acts 29 Network and serving as a consultant to churches, denominations, and colleges to help produce workers for the harvest. But they do not want men who want to be trendy or hip; nor do they want men who simply change the style, form, or elements of the service. What good is really accomplished if the only shifts are from large to intimate, or from cognitive to experiential, or from keyboards to guitars, or from slick to authentic? All those changes are window dressing. The church needs men who will address the church's unique function—men with theological rigor, who love God, will think like missionaries, and who do what works in their areas to proclaim the gospel. God-pleasers, not men-pleasers. Men who will stand up and proclaim the truth, whether their audience wants to hear it or not. Men who love God enough, and his people enough, to get "in their face" if necessary and speak the truth in love.

The Changing Role of the Expert

One of my first preaching assignments after graduating from high school was in Fieldton, Texas, where I preached to a small, country church. I arrived early and sat in

the auditorium where the adult Sunday school class met, while I waited for the service to begin. During the class, there were some questions over the meaning of a passage of Scripture, so the teacher, a man in his sixties, looked at me and asked, "Preacher, what does this verse mean?" I was only seventeen years old at the time. I had two months of college and an impressive track record of two other sermons under my belt, but I was the preacher of the day, and that pulled some weight with these people. I was the "expert." I gave them my answer, and they must have liked it just fine, since I preached for them another half dozen times while they were looking for a pastor.

Today it isn't unusual for a person half my age to question something I say, and I don't take offense at it because I don't have exclusive access to information. I'm not the expert with the final word on the matter. Besides, I know I could be wrong.

Over the past twenty years, the role of experts has changed from giving the final word on something to becoming a source of information so someone else can make a decision. Two major cultural shifts have made this change: one is the rejection of absolute truth and the other is the decentralization of information.

PC Truth

In his book *The New Absolutes*, William Watkins concludes, "Roughly three out of four Americans claimed they embraced relativism and opposed absolutism."[4] In 1997, George Barna found that "50 percent of Christians and 25 percent of non-Christians said that there are moral truths which are unchanging, that truth is not relative to the circumstances." More startling is that "16-percent report that whatever works in their life is the only truth that they know."[5]

Is our culture correct? Is it correct to say there are no absolute truths? I think the statement itself is a contradiction. It purports an absolute truth while denying its existence. To be truly politically correct, the proponents of relativism should say, "From my perspective and understanding there doesn't seem to be any objective truth, but from your perspective and understanding there could be."

On July 6, 2000, Hugh Downs, guest host on *Larry King Live*, led a roundtable discussion "Who is Jesus? And why is there such a fascination with that question now?" Among his guests was Rabbi Shmuley Boteach, dean of Oxford L'chaim Society. During the discussion, Boteach said, "Jesus was a great teacher, a very ethical, moral, human being— perhaps in our opinion, not a prophet, but certainly a phenomenal teacher, and Christianity is a great world religion. . . . And while I agree he is a great light, once we say he is the only light, this is what leads to all kinds of spiritual racism and a division between Jews and Christians."[6]

Shrewdly, Boteach shrouded his message in politically correct terms and yet managed to take a jab or two at Christianity, while appearing very open-minded. Frankly, I don't believe Rabbi Boteach when he speaks highly of Jesus and Christianity. If he really thought Jesus was a great teacher, wouldn't he follow his teaching? How can he call Jesus ethical and moral and accuse his followers of being spiritual racists for teaching what Jesus taught?

Filling the Vacuum

So how do we proclaim a truth that is unchanging and absolute to a culture where the overwhelming majority of the unchurched don't believe in absolute truth? We begin by realizing that sometimes our message will offend people. "I don't believe in insulting for the sake of Christ," says

Mark Driscoll. "But there is a reason they killed Christ, and it wasn't because they didn't like his message of successful living. It was because he spoke with authority." Instead of trying not to hurt people's feelings, we should just tell people the truth and do so with the authority Christ gave us in Matthew 28:18–20. Why can't we just proclaim the truth and let it compete with the other so-called truths in the marketplace of ideas? Since the gospel is absolute truth, it doesn't need defending, but it does need proclaiming—with a gentle spirit.

This is what Dan Kimball, pastor of Vintage Faith Church, did when a resident assistant of the University of California at Santa Cruz invited him to be a part of an open forum on Christianity. UC Santa Cruz isn't a typical college. Until 2000, they didn't give letter grades. Their bathrooms are coed; they have a large homosexual population, and their politics are liberal—very liberal. It was just a few weeks after Proposition 22 passed, a ballot measure that defined marriage as "between a man and a woman," that Kimball went to his first meeting. The overriding issue was, not surprisingly, homosexuality. "But people have these feelings," one participant said. "Why would God give us these feelings and not expect us to act on them?" Gently Kimball commented, "Some people have violent tendencies too, but that doesn't mean violence is OK."

In response to the questions, Kimball read passages from Leviticus and Romans that made clear that homosexuality was a sin, not just an alternative lifestyle, but he didn't bring his message with a condescending tone. Kimball didn't just quote Scripture; he talked about some homosexual friends

he's had—a man he toured Israel with, one of his room-
mates when he was playing with a rockabilly punk band in
England, and a former employer. In reflecting on the
exchange, Kimball says, "I hope the participants will say,
'You know, this guy absolutely said that homosexuality is a
sin, but he had heart and wasn't yelling at us. He had some
friends who were gay, and maybe he understands us.'"

"The great thing about postmodernity is the vacuum
that exists for truth," Kimball says, "and we have the privi-
lege and opportunity to fill it." In an editorial for *On
Mission*, Henry Blackaby wrote, "This is our greatest hour as
Christians. The world's values have failed, and many know
this well—with great brokenness and pain! People are
searching for what is true, stable, real, and safe." He continued, "People sense a spiritual vacuum in their lives, and they
know the world does not have real and certain answers for
them."[7] This is not a time for the church to be fearful but a
time to be faithful and fill the vacuum for truth left in an age
when people no longer believe in absolute truth.

The apostle Paul leveraged a relativistic culture at Mars
Hill by filling a vacuum for truth. Athens was polytheistic,
with statues to gods everywhere. In Athens "it was easier to
meet a god than a man."[8] They even erected a statue to the
"unknown god," just in case they missed one. A message of
monotheism would be the last thing they would want to
hear, yet that is the message Paul proclaimed. The sight of
intelligent, educated people seduced by the lie of relativism
inspired Paul to speak. Paul did not react; instead he followed a definite plan of action. He went to the synagogue
and began reasoning with the Jews and God-fearers, then to

the marketplace and presented the gospel to whomever would listen.

To the Jews who believed Jesus was a criminal worthy of crucifixion, he preached, "Jesus is the Messiah, whom God raised from the dead." Paul left the synagogue and preached in the marketplace, to an audience that did not recognize the validity of absolute truth. Significantly, his message didn't change. It was still "Jesus and the resurrection"; all that changed was his approach. Paul's message was absolute, but his approach was relative.

Paul was invited to speak at the Acropolis, a court charged with oversight of public morals—the cultural elite of the day. He found a place of common ground—their "unknown god"—and he proclaimed that God to them. He quoted their poets, but he talked about his God. What happened? Most turned away, but Acts 17:33 gives the names of some who believed. Paul's message didn't change; all that changed was his approach.

Decentralization of Information

Another reason for the changing role of the expert is the decentralization of information. Experts no longer have exclusive access to information.

We left the hospital with our oldest son twelve hours after his birth, but we were back in just a few days when he developed jaundice. We were young and scared. I asked the doctor a thousand questions, and when it became apparent to me that he was tiring of my grilling, I asked him for access to the hospital's medical library so I could find out more about the disease. That sent him over the edge. "Your baby is going to be fine," he said. "He'll be out of here in a few days." He closed his chart and left the room.

Part of the doctor's impatience with me had to do with my overreaction to my son's hospitalization and my persistent questioning. But another part of it was the times. In the early 1980s doctors were "experts"—the holders of exclusive information. We had to trust them whether we found them trustworthy or not because they were educated and we weren't. Last year I took our youngest son to the urgent care center because he had a persistent cough. When the doctor was finished examining him, she gave me her diagnosis and a couple of options for treatment, and then she asked, "What would you like me to do?"

I don't think the difference between the two encounters can be explained away by the differences in the doctors' bedside manners. Times have changed. Doctors are no longer the holders of exclusive information, and more of them are encouraging patients to participate in decision making. The Internet has decentralized information; knowledge is no longer held by an exclusive club of "experts"; anyone with Internet access can visit a medical library. Doctors are still crucial, and no one would argue otherwise; but our perception of them has changed: they are no longer gods in white coats. In a column for *Newsweek*, Anna Quindlen reacts to the news that hormone replacement therapy could do more harm than good. She writes, "The day of the Mdeity should be over; doctors have acted like little gods because patients have treated them as though they were. The woman who looks to a doctor to dictate rather than advise may wind up with treatment that she lives to regret. Or perhaps doesn't."[9]

Quindlen clearly articulates current culture's overall reaction to experts. We no longer blindly follow them; instead they are resources we use in gathering information before we make our final decision. We treat them as a "life-line" to ask them what they think before we give Regis our "final answer."

Do You Have Something Caught in Your Throat?

In 1997, a radiologist gave me a CAT scan in preparation for a second surgery to move my paralyzed vocal chord into the phonation position so I could speak. The first surgery did not result in a good speaking voice, so I flew to Nashville to have Dr. Netterville try to correct the problem. The radiologist did not know why the doctor ordered the CAT scan and, when he saw the implant in my larynx, he was concerned that I had a foreign body stuck in my larynx. So he asked me, "Have you had some kind of surgery on your throat?"

"Yes," I said. The quality of my voice would definitely give my speech problem away. I spoke in a raspy whisper. "When a surgeon performed a right thyroid lobectomy on me last spring, he tapped on my recurrent laryngeal nerve with his scalpel, resulting in vocal chord paralysis. A few months later another surgeon inserted a silastic implant in my larynx to try to mediate the paralyzed chord in the phonation position but was unsuccessful, so I'm here to have the surgery redone."

"Oh, that explains what I saw when I looked at your CAT scan," he said, and then he asked me, "Are you a doctor?" "No," I replied, "not the kind you mean anyway. I just read a lot." Today you don't have to be a doctor to gain access to medical information. The same thing applies to every discipline. Experts no longer have exclusive access to information. And it applies to the church too.

Just think about the impact on the church of printing the Bible in the vernacular of the fifteenth century. With the mass distribution of Scripture, the Reformation occurred. Today people can read multiple translations online. They can gain access to a theological reference library and find out the meaning of an original Greek word without ever sitting in a seminary classroom. Pastors no longer have exclusive access to theological information. They don't tell people what to believe. They may explain their beliefs and provide information that their listeners can use to make up their own minds, but they don't tell people what to believe. Instead of having an attitude of "I'm right about this, listen to what I have to say, learn from me and accept my teaching at face value," my attitude has become "here's what I've come to believe, and here's why I believe it; now you need to make up your mind what you believe." Instead of being someone who tells others what they should believe, I've become a guide who helps people discover truth on their own.

askmeyourquestion.com

I get a lot of e-mail from strangers because of my ministry with www.freshministry.org. Usually the questions are from ministerial students doing research for a paper or from Christians wanting guidance for their walk. As much as I can, I try to answer all the e-mails I get. Recently I received this e-mail from Michelle:

> *I read your article entitled, "It's Only Sex." You quote Hebrews 13:4 as proof that the only acceptable method of having sex is within the context of marriage. However, the passage you mentioned only states that marriage should be honored and that fornicators will be judged. This is not a statement that sex outside of marriage is fornication. In fact, Leviticus chapter 18 clearly lists all the instances of immoral sex, yet nowhere is sex between two unmarried people condemned. Could you please point out where the Bible clearly and specifically states that two unmarried people who engage in sexual relations are "fornicating"?*

Her question left me scratching my head. I mean, any Christian would understand the importance of waiting until marriage to have sex. I know that not all Christians wait for marriage to have sex, but I'd never heard one justifying his behavior by arguing about the meaning of the word *fornication*.

In my reply I pointed out that the dictionary defines the word *fornication* as "unmarried people having sexual intercourse" and that the Greek word used has a broad meaning for anyone who has any improper sexual relations. I showed her that Paul used the same word in 1 Corinthians 7:1–2 and that avoiding fornication was one reason he encouraged marriage. "There is a direct contrast here between holy sex (married) and fornication (unmarried)," I wrote. Then to help her understand the Old Testament passage she cited, I wrote, "The key to understanding Leviticus 18 is verses 28–29. This is a listing of the types of sex that should result in a person's being exiled from the community. That doesn't mean it is God's will for other types of sex, just that these types should result in being exiled."

In this communication I saw my role as providing some information for a person, and her role was to decide what to believe. I didn't tell her what to believe; I just told her what I believe. We e-mailed back and forth a couple more times as she struggled with the definition of fornication as sex between two unmarried people. I continued to wonder why she was struggling with the meaning of this word. Finally, I wrote this to her to prompt her to pray and to invite the Lord to speak to her about the issue: "Ultimately, what I think is unimportant. One day we both will give account to our Creator for the way we lived, based upon his revealed word. I suppose what I would leave you with is an encouragement to discover what God's will is for your life and those you influence with your beliefs."

Her final response helped me to understand her situation: "Personally, I'm a spiritual atheist, so discovering the 'will' of the supreme being of any religion is irrelevant for me, but thank you for your kind words. I needed a more 'Christian' perspective for a paper I am writing regarding problems with the Bible, and I am very grateful to you for giving me one." Now it made sense to me. She wasn't a conflicted Christian wanting advice; she was an atheist, trying to discredit the teachings of the Scripture. But now I had another question that bothered me, Why did she hide her identity until the end of our dialogue? Inquiring minds want to know, so I asked. Here was her reply:

As for your question, the fear of receiving an unkind or judgmental response was what prompted me to intentionally leave my beliefs out of the initial e-mail. If I had told you up front that I was a spiritual atheist, I would have had a much better chance of receiving a response that was more proselytizing than anything else (not always true, but generally). In fact, now that I think about it, I just wouldn't do that because I would be setting myself up for potential threats of eternal damnation and a lot of preaching. I wanted a straightforward response, one you might give to a fellow Christian, which is exactly what I got. It was far more productive and informational for me than an e-mail trying to convert me, which may not have answered my question at all.

I'm not sure if my answer would have been different if I had known her religious beliefs up front, but I do know it would have been different if I considered myself an expert who is supposed to tell other people what to believe. She would have gotten exactly what she expected—a judgmental response. Decentralization of information doesn't mean people don't want to listen to experts; it just means they want to make the final decision about what to believe. The more I think about it, today's climate is a healthy environment for the doctrine of the priesthood of the believer to flourish. And since I'm a firm believer in soul competency, I'm more than happy to be a spiritual adviser or guide instead of a judge. Who knows, if we make the shift, the day may come when the unchurched will come to think of the church as helpful and kind, instead of judgmental and critical.

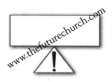

Fulcrum Point 6

Get Multi

Brian Kersey's grandfather was a founding member of a church in their California community, and his parents were active members. Kersey was very active in the youth group, leading the youth choir and going on mission trips. "He was the strongest leader in my youth group at that time," said Jack Miller, his former youth pastor.

While preparing for a mission trip to an Indian reservation, Miller trained all the youth in door-to-door evangelism. He polled the youth after the training and asked them, "Who would you like to go door-to-door with on the trip?" Brian Kersey's name was mentioned the most. Other leadership polls Miller took pointed in the same direction. Kersey was universally accepted as the leader of the youth group. When Kersey went off to college, he slowly dropped out of church. He went whenever he was asked to sing or play the drums, but on the Sundays he didn't have a place to perform, he didn't leave the dorm room at the Christian university he attended. Twenty years later he's still out of church. Sadly enough his childhood church disbanded because of a sharp decline in attendance. As it turned out, he wasn't the church's future. He dropped out of the Future Church. And he's not alone.

For years I've heard church leaders refer to teenagers as "our church's future," but they are only our future if they stay with the church when they become adults. A large percentage of them don't. "The irony is that while young adulthood is an intense time of spiritual seeking, it is the time of least church involvement. This is an acute problem for the church. Nearly 80 percent of persons in church youth groups jump ship after high school graduation."[1] Why are churches losing their young? Well, for one thing, not all those in the youth group are fully integrated into the church. They have an identity with the youth group but not necessarily with the church. Most churches segregate the youth from the rest of the church body into an activity-rich environment. The youth group numbers swell because of the activities, but many of the new youth feel no allegiance to the church; their commitment is to their friends or to the youth group. When they are too old to attend the activities, most of them fall away from the church altogether.

One of the many things I love about Dan Kimball's book *The Emerging Church: Vintage Christianity for New Generations* is the margin notes, written by other Christian thinkers whom he asked to interact with his text. In a section about Dan's metamorphosis from a modernist youth minister to a pastor for emerging generations, Mark Osteicher wrote, "Contrary to much of our current thinking about the importance of powerful youth ministries to the lifelong spiritual development of future adults, research proves otherwise: a teenager who attends a church's worship service on a regular basis and does not attend youth group is more likely to continue to attend church worship services as an adult than a teen who is active in youth group but doesn't attend worship services with other age groups."[2]

Matt Brown, founding pastor of Sandals in Riverside, California says, "Churches need to change their philosophy of youth ministry from activity-driven to small groups that disciple." Instead of the youth group being an appendage to the church, the youth can become dedicated Christ followers who are woven into the fabric of the church, ministering alongside everyone else. Mark Driscoll, pastor of Mars Hill Fellowship in Seattle, says the reason we lose our youth when they enter young adulthood is "the same reason eighteen-year-old kids don't shop at Toys-R-Us anymore. If the church is providing goods and services to self-centered Christian kids, and sort of holding their hands, as soon as they become adults, they say 'these goods and services no longer fit me.' They come back when they have kids that need those goods and services. That is contrary to the biblical pattern of people like Jeremiah, Isaiah, and Daniel, who were teenagers doing the work of God."

The biblical pattern is that youth are the church of today, not the church of tomorrow, and they need to be included in the heart and soul of the church. But the issue is bigger than generational. The Future Church is multi-generational, but it is also multiethnic and multicultural.

"A Place to Call Home"
Parkview Community Church, Glen Ellyn, Illinois

While the musicians tune their instruments, Pastor Ray Kollbocker looks over the order of worship. The first service

would begin in about thirty minutes with intense celebration, then move into a reflective mood. They would have drama, a sermon, and then more music. Parkview Community Church's style of worship isn't traditional. It isn't contemporary. It isn't blended either. It is thematic. "It doesn't matter to us whether we do hymns or brand-new hot-off-the-CD songs," Kollbocker says. "What matters to us is that they are building off the theme of the morning."

It wasn't always that way. Kollbocker arrived at First Baptist Church of Glen Ellyn, Illinois, in 1995 and was greeted by seventy-two people his first Sunday. (Today they are pushing 600.) Like many churches at that time, First Baptist was basically a traditional church trying to be up-to-date. The order of worship included a few 1980s praise choruses, but it really wasn't contemporary. The church didn't know who they were. Ministering under the shadow of several large churches, including Willow Creek Community Church, it was easy for the church to feel inadequate. "The folks couldn't help comparing themselves to other churches.

We couldn't really compete with these churches," Kollbocker says. "It was almost like an adolescent with a bad self-image."

After a retreat with church leaders, Kollbocker concluded that the church needed to change two things: their name and their direction. Their name, though prestigious, was a barrier to reaching people from adjacent communities. Glen Ellyn is an affluent city, and using the name of the town in the name of the church was negative to those who lived in the surrounding towns. The people they surveyed said, "I probably wouldn't fit in." And since 60 percent of the county is Catholic, the word *Baptist* was also negative. Within five months of Kollbocker's arrival, the church changed its name to Parkview Community Church—a fitting name since they are surrounded on three sides by a park. But they did more than change their name. Purpose emerged from their introspection. They wrote a purpose statement, mission statement, and a philosophy of ministry that guides them to this day.

Parkview's worship service is its primary "door into the church." But it isn't a seeker service. Their worship isn't a slick, professional performance for people to sit back and enjoy. Kollbocker wants the people to encounter God. And the worship can be intense. "Our goal is to teach the truth without compromise, to be ourselves and worship God in a style that we like," Kollbocker says. "We're not trying to be something we're not or hiding who we are." The purpose of worship isn't to make people feel good. "We are here to impact our ministry context with truth, to see God change lives and worship God in a way that is real."

Coming Home

This will be a good service, Kollbocker thought. As he looked up from his notes, he noticed a well-dressed African-American man milling around the foyer. "I'll be back in just a minute," Kollbocker said to the band. "There's a visitor in the foyer I want to meet." Sounds of the band faded as Pastor Ray left the auditorium to welcome the guest. "Hello, I'm Ray," Kollbocker said as he extended his right hand. The man responded with a tentative handshake, "Yeah, I know who you are," he said. "My name is Ed."

"Have you been here before?" Kollbocker asked. "Sure. Actually, I was looking for Patrick and the homeless guys. Do you know where they are?" That was the first week the church was using their new temporary buildings, and several small groups were meeting in new locations. "Let me show you where they're meeting. Do you know them?" Kollbocker asked. "Yeah, I was homeless," Ed responded. "God changed my life at this church, and I'm not turning my back on him now." Kollbocker looked closer. *Sure, I recognize him now*, he thought, but it took a second look. In many ways the transformation was such that Ed was unrecognizable.

Parkview doesn't have a ministry to the homeless. They have a ministry *with* the homeless. There is a difference. At Parkview the homeless are integrated into the fabric of the church. Some of them work on the parking crew, helping worshippers find a parking place; and others of them come early to make coffee. The change from ministry *to* the homeless to ministry *with* the homeless began in 1998. For fifteen years the church fed the homeless every

Thanksgiving, providing a traditional turkey dinner with all the trimmings to about two hundred people. The ministry was low-key—no sermons, no turn-or-burn confrontations, just a warm meal and friendly conversation.

Patrick Murnane was new in the church and wasn't planning on helping with the community Thanksgiving meal that Pastor Ray announced. It wasn't that he didn't want to; it was that he had plans to go to his sister's house for the holidays. But when he discovered the church event would end by 2:30, in time to make it to his sister's by 4:00, he signed up. That same week he got his assignment. He was to be the host for a table of homeless men that always came early every year. Little did he know how much that assignment would change his life and his church.

Things didn't go well. Around his table was quite a cast of characters. On his left were a couple of men in their fifties: Joseph, raised in a home with one Jewish and one Gentile parent, and Dominick, a man with a Catholic upbringing. On Patrick's right was Ron, a twenty-something man, and Rich, a Catholic man in his fifties. In between Ron and Rich was Steve, a slightly intoxicated man who wore a bandanna, pirate-style, over his head. Patrick did the best he could to keep a conversation going around the table. He asked questions such as, "Where's your hometown?" and "Where did you go to high school?" Small talk—no big deal. At least Patrick didn't think so.

Suddenly Steve slammed his fist on the table and shouted, "Who do you think you are? What gives you the right to ask us these questions? You may think you're better than me, but you're not!" Steve stood up. Seconds later he turned and stumbled away from the table. "Thanks a lot," Joseph said. "Because of you, somebody's gonna get hurt tonight."

Patrick felt bad and searched for Steve to apologize for offending him. He found him outside, waiting for a cab. "Steve, I want to apologize to you for ruining your Thanksgiving." Steve squinted in Patrick's direction and said, "Who are you? I've never seen you before in my life."

Humble Beginnings

Steve will never know the impact he had in Patrick's life. It was the first time he would humble himself before a homeless person, but it wouldn't be the last. He was hooked. But he wanted to get it right. He wanted to do more than feed the homeless; he wanted to open the door of the church to them. *What's going on at Thanksgiving is great,* Patrick thought, *but what about the rest of the year?* He went inside and walked over to Glenn. "Can I sit here?" he asked. Glenn smiled, nodded his head, and giggled. He didn't say much, not much Patrick could understand anyway—he was too busy wolfing down his meal. "Would you like to come back to church next Sunday?" Patrick asked. "Sure," Glenn said. "Then I'll come pick you up. Where are you going to be?"

With that conversation the ministry began. The first Sunday there was just Glenn. The next week there were two, Glenn and Kevin. The next week there were five, and the next, seven. Some weeks Patrick would drive up to 150 miles transporting the homeless around town. He helped them fill their prescriptions and made sure his "guests" had a warm meal in their stomachs before he dropped them to their "domiciles." Scores of the homeless have come to Christ through this ministry. One of them was Kevin, who attended the second week; another was Dan, who started attending a short time later. Kevin and Dan were baptized on the same Sunday in 1999—together with Patrick! Though Patrick professed faith in Christ in May 1988, he'd never followed the Lord in baptism, so it was fitting that he would be baptized on the same week as his homeless converts. After all, Patrick's ministry is *with* them, not *to* them.

Another convert was Ed.

"Get out of my way," Ed said, as he pushed his way into the van. "Move over. That's my seat. Don't you guys have a bigger van? It's too crowded in here." Ed was not a happy camper. But by now Patrick knew how to take people's outbursts in stride. During the class Ed wasn't much better. His anger was bringing down the entire group. Gently Patrick soothed Ed and slowly involved him in the discussion. "Do you have a relationship with the Lord?" Patrick asked. "Yes, I do," Ed responded. "Then would you mind closing us in prayer?" Like scales falling from his eyes, the anger left as Ed prayed.

The next week Ed was back. During the class he stretched out over several chairs and slept until someone woke him. "Come over here and sit next to me," Patrick said. "You can help me today as I teach." Several times Patrick asked him his opinion, and Ed freely gave it. After a while Ed disappeared, and Patrick didn't know what happened to him. He didn't know, that is, until he showed up one Sunday, dressed in nice clothes and asked Pastor Ray, "Where are the homeless guys meeting?"

Ed is a success story, but not every story has such a happy ending. "Some get right on the edge of success," Kollbocker says, "then go on a drinking binge." But even the "failures" are trophies of God's grace. One week the Rockford coroner's office called one of the church's deacons to identify a body. The only form of identification the man had on his body was the deacon's name and phone number. It was Dan, the other homeless man who was baptized with Patrick. Today Dan isn't homeless, and he doesn't sleep on the streets anymore. Because of a profession of faith he made at Parkview, he now lives in a place Christ prepared for him.

Ambiance

Parkview has an unusual ambiance. There are guys sleeping on the floor or smoking outside, and they smell. It can be quite a sight to visitors. The first time the Morgans walked into the building, they had to navigate through a cloud of smoke in the main hallway. What kind of a place is this where you have to walk through smoke to get to church? Not exactly a positive first impression. But by the time they took their seats, they realized, this is a good thing; this is the place where these people should be. "They are still there three years later," Kollbocker says. The church accepts all comers. "You don't have to come in a suit. You can come in tattered clothes. We have downtown Chicago executives sitting next to homeless people."

Parkview hasn't targeted any homogeneous unit. "We don't give a rip where they are from, how old they are, single, divorced, homeless, rich," Kollbocker says. "We're just looking for spiritually disconnected people." Spiritually disconnected people are in every sociographic and demographic grouping—a lesson associate pastor Steve Tomlinson learned during a conversation with Brenda, a woman in her twenties. "How did you end up at Parkview?" Tomlinson asked. "I used to attend another church and worship with the 'happy shiny people' until I just could not keep the act up anymore," Brenda responded. "When I came to Parkview, I noticed that your building was old. Then I noticed that the person sitting next to me was obviously homeless. Then I realized that this is a place where broken people can come, and I've been here ever since."

As Steve listened to Brenda's story, he discovered that her husband had walked away from the Lord a few years before, and she feared for the spiritual development of her two young children. She needed to keep them in church, even if their father wouldn't go with them, but she couldn't stomach the thought of going to a place where she had to "have it all together." Brenda felt more comfortable sitting next to a homeless man in a church where she could be herself than next to the "happy shiny people" where she felt she had to put on airs.

"It doesn't matter who you are or what you look like," Kollbocker says. "This is an embracing place where you can be real, where you can hurt or cry—a place where you can repent."

One Sunday the pastor baptized ten people who repented of their sins and committed their lives to Christ. Six of them had homes to go to after the service, but four of them didn't. But they all have something in common: they have a church, a place all of them call home.

Inclusiveness

My brothers formed a club when I was five years old. They had a neat clubhouse (an old, dusty toolshed), a thriving membership (a couple of other  kids from the neighborhood), and a membership policy (you had to be at least six years old to join). Obviously, this left me out. "I can't wait until next year," I said. "Then I'll be old enough to join your club." My brother was quick to reply, "By then you'll have to be seven to join."

Now don't start feeling sorry for me. The truth is, I was a scrawny little tagalong brother. I'm sure my older brothers got tired of having to walk slower so I could keep up or watching me while Mom and Dad went somewhere. They just wanted some peace and quiet. But I've never forgotten that feeling. It's the same feeling I felt in junior high when I was the last to be picked to be on a dodgeball team and the same feeling I felt in high school when a girl couldn't go out with me because she said she "had to wash her hair on Friday night." I'm happy to be unique, but I don't want to be different, not if it means being excluded. Perhaps that's the reason it is so natural to hang around people just like me—because I know I'll fit in.

Generational Targeting

In an age where a core doctrine of the culture is multiculturalism, diversity, and inclusiveness, can a church be selective in whom it reaches? Can it be target-driven? In 1986 Dieter Zander launched a church to cater to young adults, and in the process began the first Gen X church in America. The church's mission was to reach "betweeners"—people who didn't fit in the family section of the church because of their marital status or into the youth ministry because of their age. The "betweeners" didn't fit in with the established clubs, so they started their own, and the young adults flocked to sign up. It was Marketing 101: discover what the target group wants, develop a product that meets their needs, and market the product directly to them. It was, after all, the 1980s, and that was the conventional wisdom of the time. And it worked. Before Zander left to join the staff at Willow Creek, the church grew to twelve hundred in attendance. The average age of attenders was twenty-six. They'd hit their target!

Is that the solution to young adults feeling left out? Should they just start their own exclusive club? If they do, will what they create ever be the church? "Some churches are really just college ministries that call themselves churches," says Mark Driscoll, pastor of Mars Hill Fellowship in Seattle. "They don't have members, discipline, elders, or sacrificial giving. They are extending youth ministry into the thirties. They are just providing another 'business' where disgruntled 'customers' can get 'goods and services'—perpetuating the narcissistic cycle indefinitely."

For the longest time I have to admit that I thought the issue was generational. Five or six years ago, publishing houses were spitting out generational ministry books faster than I could read them. In one year publishers sent me review copies of their books showing how to reach the Builder, Boomer, Buster, and Bridger generations. These books were like gremlins, and someone must have added water to them because they multiplied, and before I knew it, I was overwhelmed. It couldn't be that hard. In those days we thought the only way to reach young adults was to target them as a group and sculpt a service to reach them. But times have changed, and that's not what's happening today.

About that time Kelly Williams launched Vanguard in Colorado Springs. He says, "Initially we targeted Generation X. But not now. The oldest person in our church is seventy-five. As far as age is concerned, our saturation is younger, but we have all ages that any traditional church would have."

About a thousand miles away, Ron Martoia, founding pastor of Westwinds Community Church in Jackson, Michigan, was discovering the folly of generational targeting. He was warned by people in their sixties, "Don't make this generational. I've been looking for something like this my whole life." One of the fastest-growing segments at Westwinds calls themselves the Ameners—ageless, mature, empty nesters—people predominantly in their fifties.

Today Sandals in Riverside, California, reports that the fastest-growing group in the church is people in their thirties and fifties. "I would venture to say it would be very difficult to categorize Sandals as a 'Gen X Church,'" says Nathan Brown, administrative pastor.

Mars Hill Fellowship in Seattle describes themselves as "a family with members of all ages, the majority of whom are in their twenties." Mark Driscoll, the pastor, reports that the "oldest attender is ninety-four."

Graceland, in Santa Cruz, was launched to reach "betweeners" but has expanded to include people of all ages. Pastor Dan Kimball says, "The personality [of the service] is appealing to more than just young adults."

George, a man in his seventies, responded to a flyer for a new Southern Baptist church in Stockton, California, and came to one of their first services. "I've been to several Southern Baptist services in my time," George told lead pastor Roger Williams III, "and this is a step up."

When Chris Kratzer started Quest 419 in Tampa Bay, Florida, he was targeting a demographic age group, Generation X. But he soon learned he should target a cultural mind-set. "One guy we reached in his early sixties has been through several marriages and has a teenage daughter. His life was racked with guilt, but through the ministry of Quest, he has discovered God's forgiveness and release from his shame."

What I hear these people saying, young and old alike, isn't that they want to be targeted. I hear them saying that they want to be valued and included. Today Zander is planting another church, this time in San Francisco. But he isn't targeting Gen Xers. Instead, he is launching a multigenerational church where young adults are valued and welcomed.

A Wild Card

In the early nineties, I attended a retreat with other church leaders at Big Bear, California, to learn how better to reach young adults. At the retreat there were the usual speakers, times of worship, and brainstorming sessions, but the most valuable time for me was an informal listening session. We broke up into small groups comprised of church leaders like myself, but each group had a wild card element in it—at least one young adult. And the young adult was the leader. We listened; the young adult spoke. In many ways that young adult changed my ministry that day. Really, my quest to reach young adults began around that picnic table in the mountains. Basically, his message was, "Don't treat me like a kid. If I'm old enough to vote and to die for my country, why am I not old enough to be an usher in your church or serve on a committee?"

He didn't want to be an attender. He wanted to be a participant—a fully vested member. "Young adults do not want to be treated like adolescents. They want to be challenged to do something more," Driscoll says. "We don't treat you like a child [at Mars Hill]." The need isn't for an exclusive club for young adults. It is for a place where young adults are valued and welcomed—a place where they are challenged to do something and to contribute to the welfare of the church.

Future Churches are effectively reaching young adults and may be composed predominantly of young adults. But they are not exclusively for young adults. As the churches mature, they are becoming multigenerational, a place where the older can mentor the younger, and the younger can invigorate their elders—a church where Paul and Timothy minister together and Paul can say to his younger fellow-believer, "Don't let anyone look down on you because you are young, but set an example for the believers in speech, in life, in love, in faith and in purity" (1 Tim. 4:12 NIV). This is a church where the older women can teach the younger women how to care for their husbands and their children (Titus 2:3–4), not a hip church or a church with flair but a biblical church that welcomes and embraces everyone, regardless of age. And regardless of ethnicity.

Unity in Diversity

It isn't just about age. One of my earliest memories of church was something my preschool teacher said to me in a rural Texas church. "Don't put that nickel in your mouth," she said, "a [expletive deleted] may have touched it." That wasn't the only time I've heard the "n" word in church. When I was in high school, the church I attended was debating whether to close down the Spanish mission and absorb the few attenders left into the Anglo congregation. One of the deacons secured the floor of the business meeting and said, "If we let the Mexicans in, the next thing you know, the [expletive deleted] will want to follow." I don't recall how the vote went that day, but I do remember the duplicity of a church that talked about loving their neighbors while refusing to welcome those neighbors into their church unless they were white.

Prejudice isn't always so overt. Sometimes it is more subtle than that. All of the active members of Timothy

Urbany's Sunday school class at Eastborough Church in Colorado Springs were white, middle-class, and married with children. They were birds of a feather that flocked together. Urbany longed for his class to be more diverse, more accepting of others, so he invited a Christian friend from work to attend his class to help him evaluate their potential for growth. She was a single, young black woman. She arrived early and helped herself to a doughnut and some coffee. She participated in the discussion and did her best to make herself at home. No one spoke to her.

The next week Urbany explained to the class who the young woman was and reported to his class her impressions of the class. They were stunned that none of the members of their loving class reached out to her to make her feel welcome and wanted. It was almost as if they didn't even notice her. Really, the class's reaction was predictable. Most people naturally tend to gravitate toward people they have something in common with. In many ways the church isn't much different from lunchtime at any middle school. The "pocket protector" kids sit at one table, the "jocks" at another, and the "princesses" at another. We tend to cluster with people like us. That event jolted the class and woke them up to their subtle prejudice. Urbany's class is still fairly homogeneous, but later they did assimilate a person into their fellowship who closely resembled the woman who previously visited them. They are learning to minister to whomever the Lord gives them, not just to people like them.

This is a lesson every church needs to learn. If we won't listen to culture as it preaches diversity, maybe we will listen to Scripture: "There is neither Jew nor Greek, slave nor free,

male nor female, for you are all one in Christ Jesus" (Gal.
3:28 NIV).

Will You Be My Neighbor?

In the wake of the most recent shuttle disaster, I spent
some time reflecting about the day Dad called us all into the
living room to watch history in the making. All Neil
Armstrong did was take a small step, but Dad was right; it
was history. It was a "giant leap for mankind." He'd crossed
a barrier, a wall that changed the world.

Since that night I've always been keenly aware when
I was watching history unfold. There was the brisk fall
evening in 1988 when Kirk Gibson limped up to the plate
in the World Series. His bat had propelled the Dodgers into
the Series against the A's, but it didn't look like he'd be able
to help them now. But in a gutsy move, Lasorda sent the
injured slugger to the plate with the game on the line.
Gibson knocked the ball out of the park and hobbled
around the bases to lead his team to victory that day and
provided a spark to his team to take the Series. Who would
have thought that knocking a ball over a wall would have
that kind of impact?

One of my favorite history moments on TV happened
the year before. President Ronald Reagan stood beside the
Brandenburg Gate in West Berlin, Germany, on June 12,
1987, and said, "Come here to this gate! Mr. Gorbachev.
Open this gate! Mr. Gorbachev. Tear down this wall!" And
before you know it, the wall came down, and when it did,
the world changed forever. I like this moment the best for
two reasons. One, because of the impact those few words

"tear down this wall" had on human history. It reminds me that what we say really can make a difference. But another reason I like it is because, in my mind, it underscores Paul's words, "For He Himself is our peace, who made both groups into one, and broke down the barrier of the dividing wall" (Eph. 2:14 NASB). Jesus tore down the wall that separated the Jews from the Gentiles, and that definitely made it possible for all people everywhere to get along.

Our real heroes aren't the ones who build the walls. They are the ones that scale them or, better yet, tear them down. So why is it so easy to let my prejudices build an artificial wall between me and neighbor?

The parable of the Good Samaritan helps us deal with that question. Perhaps only John 3:16 and Psalm 23 are better known by the public at large than the parable of the Good Samaritan.

> And behold, a certain lawyer stood up and put Him to the test, saying, "Teacher, what shall I do to inherit eternal life?" And He said to him, "What is written in the Law? How does it read to you?" And he answered and said, "You shall love the Lord your God with all your heart, and with all your soul, and with all your strength, and with all your mind; and your neighbor as yourself." And He said to him, "You have answered correctly; do this, and you will live." But wishing to justify himself, he said to Jesus, "And who is my neighbor?" Jesus replied and said, "A certain man was going down from Jerusalem to Jericho; and he fell among robbers, and they stripped him and beat

him, and went off leaving him half dead. And by chance a certain priest was going down on that road, and when he saw him, he passed by on the other side. And likewise a Levite also, when he came to the place and saw him, passed by on the other side. But a certain Samaritan, who was on a journey, came upon him; and when he saw him, he felt compassion, and came to him, and bandaged up his wounds, pouring oil and wine on them; and he put him on his own beast, and brought him to an inn, and took care of him. And on the next day he took out two denarii and gave them to the innkeeper and said, 'Take care of him; and whatever more you spend, when I return, I will repay you.' Which of these three do you think proved to be a neighbor to the man who fell into the robbers' hands?" And he said, "The one who showed mercy toward him." And Jesus said to him, "Go and do the same" (Luke 10:25–37 NASB).

Familiar passages, like this one, offer unique challenges and opportunities when we study them. Somehow we need to find a way to set aside our previous conclusions about the text because if we don't, we will block any new insights that we can glean from a careful, prayerful study of it. This text in particular is challenging because the Good Samaritan has become a cultural icon. The term has come to mean any stranger who performs an act of kindness. The *Oxford American Dictionary* defines a *Good Samaritan* as "someone who readily gives help to a person in distress who has no claim on him." Newswriters often use the term to denote someone who helps a stranger without regard to reward. In sum, Good Samaritans act without asking, "What's in it for me?" They do what is right, just because it is right.

At face value that's a decent definition. Unfortunately, I don't believe it goes far enough. The problem with the working definition of a Good Samaritan as someone who performs an act of kindness, beyond the fact that the teaching here is greater than that, is that it can also be skewed to be something negative. I recently read an article on www.CNN.com entitled "E-posses patrol for auction fraud." According to the article, people who've been duped using online auctions like eBay are patrolling these services to help protect others from the same types of scams that they fell prey to. Tom Mainelli, author of the article, used the term "Good Samaritans" to describe these people who are helping others on the auctions sites, but he also used terms like "overzealous do-gooders" and "kamikaze vigilantes" to describe them.[3] I don't know which of those terms best describes what the e-posses are doing on the Internet, but I do know they are not synonyms. And that is the problem: the term has lost its real meaning as it has made its way into our mainstream vocabulary. Jesus' listeners did not have our working definition of the term when they heard it. In fact, this was probably the first time a Jew ever used the two words together. In their view, *good* would never be used to describe a Samaritan.

And that is the point of this parable. A man whom Jesus' Jewish listeners despised was the one with real virtue. Not the priest. Not the Levite. It was a despised, despicable

Samaritan who was neighborly. It would surprise no one if the priest or the Levite had rendered aid, without regard for reward—that is what religious people are supposed to do. But it was an outlandish surprise that the Samaritan did. As a whole, the Jews despised Samaritans. Extrabiblical material calls them "the foolish people who dwell in Shechem," and Shechem is referred to elsewhere as a "city of fools."[4] There was a clear divide between Jews and Samaritans. Remember the words of the Samaritan woman, "How is it that You, being a Jew, ask me for a drink since I am a Samaritan woman?" (John 4:9). The text adds, "For Jews have no dealings with Samaritans."

What makes this a great parable isn't that a stranger rendered aid to a crime victim and provided long-term care for him. Rather, it is that the stranger who did it was a Samaritan. In answering the lawyer's question about being a neighbor, Jesus didn't define *neighbor* as "someone who shares your morals, interests, economic status, and religious beliefs." He didn't say that neighbors are people you feel comfortable being around. They are not "birds of a feather." A neighbor in this parable is someone you despise yet acts neighborly toward you. Prejudices can keep people from spotting a real neighbor when they see one. Whether the prejudice arises because of race, beliefs, economic status, personal appearance, or hobbies, it can force people into an "us-them" clique.

It happened in the early church. Acts 6:1 says, "Now at this time while the disciples were increasing in number, a complaint arose on the part of the Hellenistic Jews against the native Hebrews, because their widows were being overlooked in the daily serving of food." The congregation was divided in cliques. There were those who embraced the Greek language and culture, and there were those who were native Hebrews who rejected the Greek culture. These two groups were divided by their differences, and their differences stopped one group from viewing the other as neighbors—people they needed to act neighborly toward. Their prejudices got in the way.

Everyone has prejudices. The parable of the Good Samaritan teaches us to confront our prejudices, move them aside, and look at people, not dismiss them. Not focus on their race, beliefs, age, economic status, or their differences; but look past those things and see their soul. The man in this parable wasn't a lowly, foolish Samaritan. He was a neighbor. Conversely, the priest and the Levite weren't religious, good people. They were unneighborly. The crime in acting on prejudice isn't just the potential of acting violently toward someone, like the robbers, who beat the man. It is passively dismissing them and seeing them as persons undeserving of neighborly actions, like the priest and the Levite did. The lawyer who asked Jesus the question came to grips with his own prejudice and admitted to Jesus that the neighbor was the one who showed mercy—the Samaritan.

Shouldn't a church that takes this parable seriously be filled with people of all races and cultures? Why would it let preferences be a barrier? Shouldn't a church that takes this parable seriously be filled with people who like all types of music, from all economic standings, and all walks of life? The only way that will happen is if the church lays aside its prejudices and takes time to look past the surface and see people's souls. Souls for whom Christ died. Souls who are our neighbors.

Will You Be My Leader?

But the question isn't just, Will we allow people different from us to come to our church? but also, Will our church ever become their church too? Will young and old alike share power? Will minorities become leaders, elders, and deacons? Will women ever have "stage time," or will they be relegated to behind-the-scenes work?

Fenton Ward, a retired pastor who attends the church I presently serve, invested his life as a missionary to the Jews and began Tarzana Baptist Chapel to reach the Los Angeles Jewish population. They did reach Jews but not exclusively. One Sunday, Ward looked up during the offering and saw that one of the ushers was a Jew, the other an Arab. Another week he noticed that one usher was a Vietnam veteran while the other was a Vietnamese refugee. Even though his target group was Jewish, his congregation was diverse. Why? Ward accepted whomever God added to his church and allowed them to lead.

Sometimes it is impossible to predict what God will do. Erwin McManus was born in El Salvador, Central America, raised in Miami, and is now pastoring Mosaic, a church in an area of Los Angeles with a heavy Hispanic population. His predecessor was Caucasian, but when McManus arrived, the church was predominantly Hispanic. Every indicator would point in the direction of growth in that population, but that hasn't been the case. One of the largest people groups God added to Mosaic is Asian. The Future Church is a place where young and old, black and white, Hispanic and Asian worship together and serve together. It is diverse.

The Future Church is a dress rehearsal for heaven, where people of all ages, colors, and backgrounds will be together—people who have one thing in common: they are wicked sinners saved by the grace of God and spending eternity worshipping him.

Tolerance

"When I was a little boy, I was very religious," said Ted Turner as he addressed religious and spiritual leaders from around the world at the Millennium World Peace Summit of the United Nations.

I was born into a Christian family, and I was raised in a Christian school. I became a Christian just like you become whatever you are exposed to as a child. I was going to be a man of the cloth. I'd be sitting out there with you, and I would have loved a life like that. I was going to be a missionary.

I studied religion. First, I studied Christianity, and later I studied the world's great religions through reading, and I was always thinking. What disturbed me is that my religious Christian sect was very intolerant—not intolerant of religious freedom for other people, but we thought that we were the only ones going to heaven. The

Catholics weren't going to heaven. The Muslims weren't going to heaven. The Hindus weren't going to heaven. The Shintoists weren't going to heaven. Nobody was going to heaven but us. I figured it wasn't even one percent of the world's population. It just confused the devil out of me because I said heaven is going to be a mighty empty place with nobody else there. So I was pretty confused and turned off by it. I said it just can't be right.[5]

For Turner, it wasn't enough that Christians fight for the right of religious freedom for all people. He wanted Christianity to disembowel itself of its core beliefs. The teachings of Turner say that everyone, regardless of what they believe, can make it to heaven. The teachings of Christ, however, don't. Jesus said, "I am the way, the truth, and the life: no man cometh unto the Father, but by me" (John 14:6 KJV). To get to a particular destination requires a specific path. If I want to fly to New York, I can't board just any plane. All planes don't lead to the same place. If I want to go to heaven, I can't follow just any religion. All religions don't lead to the same place. Narrow-minded? Perhaps. Biblical? Absolutely.

In his address Turner accurately stated the majority view of our culture. "Make any claim you want," culture says, "just don't make an exclusive claim." As confident as I am that I am right about this, I am equally convinced that more people in our culture would agree with Turner than with me. On the surface those who preach tolerance appear to be kindhearted, not wanting to hurt other people. But is it kind to tell people a lie, just to avoid hurting their feelings, even if the lie will result in their destruction? It may be tolerant, but it isn't right.

The Pot Calling the Kettle Intolerant

The core message of salvation by Christ alone isn't the only Christian message that current culture finds intolerant. How do Christians address issues such as homosexuality and abortion in a culture that is more accepting of those choices than of those who speak against them?

On June 16, 1998, Senator Trent Lott taped an interview for *The Armstrong Williams Show* on the America's Voice television network. During the interview Williams asked Lott whether he considers homosexuality a sin, and Lott replied, "Yeah, it is. You should still love that person. You should not try to mistreat them or treat them as outcasts. You should try to show them a way to deal with that problem, just like alcohol . . . or sex addiction . . . or kleptomaniacs."[6]

One Web site from the gay community featured the AP article with their headline: "Trent Lott: Hate Mongering Homophobic Christian Bigot Exposed." The page also included the word *moron* several times in reference to those who want to show love toward homosexuals and help them deal with their problem.[7]

Isn't that response a bit intolerant? Aren't those who are angry about Christianity's so-called intolerance showing extreme intolerance themselves with their reaction to it? To the cultural elite of our day, intolerance is tantamount to hate. Some even characterize the Christian message as "hate filled" because it attempts to influence the behavior of others. In effect they say, "Who do you think you are to judge me? What goes on in the privacy of my home is my business. You shouldn't judge me by my private life." But isn't calling the Christian message "hate filled" a judgment in itself? Culture's very words are violating their message of being nonjudgmental. Principal Jody McLoud of Roane County High School, Kingston, Tennessee, expressed the frustration of many on September 1, 2000, when he addressed the crowd that gathered for a football game. He said:

> It has always been the custom at Roane County
> High School football games to say a prayer and play
> the national anthem to honor God and country. Due
> to a recent ruling by the Supreme Court, I am told
> that saying a prayer is a violation of Federal case law.
>
> As I understand the law at this time, I can use this
> public facility to approve of sexual perversion and call
> it an alternate lifestyle, and if someone is offended,
> that's OK. I can use it to condone sexual promiscuity
> by dispensing condoms and calling it safe sex. If some-
> one is offended, that's OK. I can even use this public
> facility to present the merits of killing an unborn baby
> as a viable means of birth control. If someone is
> offended, no problem. I can designate a school day as
> Earth Day and involve students in activities to reli-
> giously worship and praise the goddess, Mother Earth,
> and call it ecology. I can use literature, videos and
> presentations in the classroom that depict people with
> strong, traditional, Christian convictions as simple

*minded and ignorant and call it enlightenment.
However, if anyone uses this facility to honor God
and ask Him to bless this event with safety and good
sportsmanship, Federal case law is violated.*

*This appears to be inconsistent at best, and at
worst, diabolical. Apparently, we are to be tolerant
of everything and anyone except God and His
commandments.*

While it is obvious to me that the cultural elite is guilty
of being intolerant while preaching the virtues of tolerance,
I'm not so quick to completely dismiss their criticisms of the
Christian community. Christians can be condescending. We
can be judgmental. We can be intolerant of anyone who disagrees
with us. There is plenty of historical evidence ranging
from the inquisitions to the crusades that Christians
don't always act Christlike.

Sowing and Reaping

In many ways Christians are being repaid for what we've
dished out. Professor William A. Dembski is a leading proponent
of Intelligent Design, a school of thought that
teaches that the universe is a product of mindful planning
rather than random chance. Although he is an evangelical
Christian, his work does not name God as the designer of
the universe. Dembski used to run Baylor's Center for
Complexity, Information, and Design, but after a conference
on the subject, the faculty senate asked the university's
president to end all Intelligent Design initiatives on campus.
Biologists on campus boycotted Dembski's conference,

while others sent out bogus letters from Baylor "disinviting" scheduled speakers.[8]

Christians complain that we can't teach creationism in public schools today, but wasn't it Christians who said to the evolutionists last century that they couldn't teach their beliefs? Christian intolerance is what led to the Scopes monkey trials and the current prohibition against teaching creationism. Today I'd be happy to allow the evolutionists to teach their theories if Christians could teach theirs in the same classroom. Why not let teachers present both views and let the student decide?

Becoming more tolerant doesn't mean that Christians must become soft on sin and turn our backs on injustice. Jesus was soft on sinners but hard on sin. Remember his encounter with the woman caught in the act of adultery? The scribes and Pharisees brought her before Jesus, claiming they had caught her in the very act of adultery. They asked him if they should stone her as the law prescribed. Here's what Jesus said to them and to her:

"He who is without sin among you, let him be the first to throw a stone at her." And again He stooped down, and wrote on the ground. And when they heard it, they began to go out one by one, beginning with the older ones, and He was left alone, and the woman, where she had been, in the midst. And straightening up, Jesus said to her, "Woman, where are they? Did no one condemn you?" And she said, "No one, Lord." And Jesus said, "Neither do I condemn you; go your way. From now on sin no more" (John 8:7–11 NASB).

Jesus judged her in that he told her to sin no more, but he wasn't judgmental or condemning.

What's Love Got to Do with It?

Jesus said, "Do not give what is holy to dogs, and do not throw your pearls before swine, lest they trample them under their feet, and turn and tear you to pieces" (Matt. 7:6 NASB). We are not to be brain-dead people who will tolerate anything. We are to be discerning, and we are to minister with a spirit of redemption, not of condemnation. Most of all, we need to examine our own hearts—a lesson I learned over twenty years ago when a retired denominational worker said to me: "Jim, I can tell you really hate sin. Maybe one day you'll learn to love sinners."

I'd really "let 'em have it" that night. People walked the aisle, and I was feeling quite good. I didn't pay much attention to his comments; after all, I was the hotshot young preacher. He didn't know what he was talking about. But if he was so wrong, why do I still remember his words twenty years later? I was right to mention hell and warn people of the judgment that awaits them. Christians can't talk about pleasant subjects exclusively. We're not spiritual anesthesiologists, helping to sedate people in their pain. People need a cure, not sedation. Yet, though my words were right, my spirit was wrong. It made me feel so right to tell others they were so wrong. This retired preacher was able to look through my words and into my heart. He pegged me.

With time I've learned to talk about judgment with a tear in my eye, not a smirk on my face. Today broken lives break my heart. Regardless of the culture's response,

Christians must tell the truth about an unrepentant sinner's eternal destiny. But courage isn't enough. We must stain our Bibles with our tears while we warn people of the place where there is "weeping and gnashing of teeth." And when they see right through us, they will encounter Christ's love, and perhaps they will accept Christ's sacrifice for their sins.

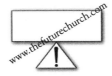

Fulcrum Point 7

Get Connected

I'm totally wired. From the day I took my first Commodore computer out of the box in the 1980s, I've been hooked. I have no idea how many computers I've owned since then. I have a private network of three computers in my office. I run two computers at a time at my desk and have the third positioned by a small conference table just in case I need to access information while counseling. My private network is also networked to other computers in the office building. The desktop computer in my office is my "mule." It has a CD burner, zip drive, tape backup, scanner, and printer hooked up to it. I call the third computer my "dino." It is the slowest and oldest of the triad. My primary computer is a laptop that I can take with me most places, but I keep it in sync with my wireless handheld that I keep with me all the time. I have a power inverter for my laptop so I can plug it in the cigarette lighter in the car and work beyond the two-hour life of the battery, and I have a spare battery so I can write anywhere—at the boardwalk, beach, a restaurant, anywhere.

I use a digital camera with a floppy disk drive so I can transfer pictures to the laptop for PowerPoint presentations or to upload to one of my Web sites. But what is really cool is the special hot-wire connection that links my digital video camera to my laptop so I can capture still images from the videotape.

ATM and credit cards are great. I rarely have to go into a place of business. I do most of my shopping over the Internet, do my banking at ATMs, and fill up my pickup at "pay at the pump" gas stations. Isn't technology wonderful? I don't have to be bothered talking to people to get things done anymore. My banker? Don't have one. The gas station attendant? Never see one. The pharmacist? I can tell you the URL to the Web site but have no idea who is filling my prescriptions. The clerk at the photo shop? I do my own processing, thank you. The printer? I can produce anything I need in my own office. I don't need a printer. I don't need anybody.

And look at all the time technology saves me! It used to be that if I wanted to work, I had to be in the office. Now I can work anywhere: in the car, at the amusement park, at the restaurant—I can work anytime I want.

Come to think of it, that's my biggest problem. It seems that the more wired I get, the more I am disconnected from the people around me. The ability to work anywhere often means I never get away from work. The fact that I don't have to see people to get things done means I'm isolated and sometimes—well, sometimes I'm lonely. I know what technology has done for my life. But there is something I don't know. I don't know what technology is doing to my soul.

"An Extra Helping of Grace"
Agape Community Church, Rio Rancho, New Mexico

Rarely do more than fifty people attend Agape Community Church in Rio Rancho, New Mexico. It's a storefront church that meets on the population-dense West Mesa, just outside of Albuquerque, surrounded by fast-growing churches. Agape doesn't minister under anybody's spotlight. It just carries out

its mission, in the obscurity of faithfulness to people who require a little extra grace to make it. Their pastor, Jim Sandell, isn't going to win the "hippest pastor of the year award" anytime soon. He's not one of those conference-speaker types with devilish good looks and an electrifying personality. Jim has a sort of wind-tossed look about him. He's a big man whose heart shines through his smile and the glint in his eyes.

As the service begins, Jim stands in the middle of the band with his twelve-string guitar strapped to his shoulder. On his right is a vocalist holding a tambourine; to his left is a keyboardist; and immediately in front of him is an overhead projector. He strums his Ovation while he gives a few announcements and then begins leading the congregation of adults, children, youth, and senior citizens in an eclectic selection of music ranging from the old hymns, campfire choruses, and current offerings. The service progresses seamlessly, transitioning from music to conversation to prayer to preaching. Sandell never leaves center stage.

The congregation fully participates. Sandell doesn't ask rhetorical questions; when he asks a question during his sermon, people from the congregation respond. In the middle of a worship set, he asks people to share praises or prayer requests, and they do. They share personal stuff—such as when a relative will get out of jail or how their damaged marriage is doing this week—the kind of prayer requests usually reserved for a small circle of friends, not the whole church. But that's the feel of Agape—a small circle of friends, friends who accept you as you are and will pray for you to become what God wants you to be.

Pilgrims Looking for Healing

Agape began the way many churches begin, from a church split. When the church wouldn't fulfill some promises they made to their new pastor, the pastor moved to another church field, and a good portion of the church split off. Sandell, the youth minister at the church, left with them. They had provisional worship services until a new church in the area agreed to sponsor them as a new work. One morning in February 1996, Jim and forty other people joined Celebration Baptist Church. Some of the people stayed with Celebration, but others began the new work in March 1996, a week after Celebration was constituted as a church. In the beginning they met on Saturday nights in Celebration's storefront; Jim led the worship and John Embry, the pastor from Celebration, preached.

In February 1997 the owners of the shopping center wanted to put in a bar two doors down from the church. Since New Mexico law prohibits opening a bar within three hundred feet of a church, they kicked out the church. Celebration moved to a Seventh Day Adventist Church in Corrales, but because Sandell's group met on Saturday night, they couldn't go with them. Agape met at another church's facilities until they found their own facility to rent. During the summer of 1997, they started having Sunday services in addition to their Saturday services, and the church called Sandell as their pastor. For most of the time, Sandell has been bivocational, working as a radio announcer during the day and devoting himself to the church on evenings and weekends. But recently he stepped out on faith and quit his day job. The church can't pay him much, and he doesn't have benefits such as health insurance, but he's willing to make the sacrifice to live out his calling.

In the winter of 2000, Sandell took his church leaders on a prayer/vision retreat, proposing either to discover God's vision for their church or to close the doors. On the retreat, they came to understand that God has a unique calling for their church—to minister to people who require "extra grace" and don't feel they fit in at most churches. "We all have a picture of what an ideal church is," Sandell says. "Agape Community Church is not that church. It isn't a church where people put on a happy face with their three-piece suits. But it is a place where people can be accepted with whatever needs they have." It is a church for people who require an extra helping of grace. "God has brought to us people who have needs, people who didn't fit in at other places. They are EGR people—Extra Grace Required," Sandell says. "They are the people who get on your nerves and are a little bit annoying. A lot of churches will cut them off after a while. When that happens, they end up here."

One such person is Janice. A lifetime of tragedy is etched on her fifty-year-old complexion. She's had four husbands and five children. Today she knows where only one of the children is and doesn't care to know where any of her husbands are; she was a battered wife. The beatings took their toll. To this day Janice suffers lingering disabilities from the abuse, compounded by an auto accident a few years later. She's a squirrelly sort of person who has a hard time finding any social equilibrium. Because of her health, Janice can't hold down a job, but she isn't lazy—quite the opposite. She is very resourceful, supporting herself by collecting junk, cleaning it up, and selling it at garage sales. One crisis after another follows in her wake. She always seems to be a few steps away from calamity and in constant need of grace—an extra portion of grace.

Janice's car was in worse shape than she was—always breaking down. Men in the church tried to stop it from overheating; they even took it to a mechanic when they couldn't fix it but to no avail. It was shot. Jim and his wife Jolene took Janice's need seriously and began looking through the *Penny Saver* to see if they could find a car that the church might be able to buy for Janice. But before they did, a member of the church handed Sandell the keys to his old car and said, "Pastor, we bought a new car this week and thought we'd give our old one to the church just in case you or someone else might need it." Jim immediately thought of Janice. Now, with the gift, she had reliable transportation, but her problems weren't over.

Janice is missing that something that most people have in their makeup that lets them know when they are acting inappropriately. If she's feeling depressed at three in the morning and needs to talk, she doesn't think twice about picking up the phone and dialing a phone number. At times the pastor reaches his wit's end with people like Janice; and when he does, he prays: "Lord, I know you've brought these people here for us to minister to. I pray for the strength to do what I can do to make a difference. And give me the extra grace I need to extend extra grace to them." Part of extending extra grace to people like Janice is not to view them as a ministry project but to see them as someone Christ has drawn to their church—a part of the family.

Velvet Hammer

Sometimes the grace required is gentle discipline. Reuben and Lynda seemed to be made for each other. They had good jobs and lived in a nice home. They had four kids between them, but they weren't married. Reuben was a Christian and thought the kids ought to be in church, so they started attending Agape. The church accepted them as they were. "They needed to belong somewhere and have someone care about them before they had to fix every aspect of their life," Sandell says. Agape welcomed them into the community and then introduced them to Christ and Christian values. With time Lynda came to faith in Christ, and the couple got married. One Sunday Reuben's mother visited from back east and said to the pastor, "I'm so glad Reuben and Lynda found a church where they could be accepted. I've been telling them what they should do, but they wouldn't listen to me. But they took it coming from you guys."

All around them, churches are growing. The church they split from has experienced explosive growth. Several new church plants in the area have blossomed, but Agape continues just to hold its own. "We haven't had a lot of growth, but we've touched a lot of lives. People come. They get whole, and then God moves them on," Sandell says.

That's what happened with Bruce and Brenda and their three girls. Like many others in Rio Rancho, Bruce worked at the Intel plant and Brenda was a stay-at-home mom—a Martha Stewart type who devoted herself totally to her family. They drifted from one church to another, finding fault with the pastor or the program. Sandell noticed that Brenda harbored bitterness even toward one particular pastor who didn't like the Dallas Cowboys and who would regularly make snide remarks about them from the pulpit. That didn't sit well with Brenda, a Cowboys fanatic, so she talked Bruce into pulling the family out of the church and going to look for another one.

Sandell gently confronted Brenda and told her she needed to make peace with her former pastor and get over this kind of pettiness. Bruce and Brenda made the appointment and reconciled with their former pastor. They stayed with Agape for over three years before changing churches. This time they didn't leave over some petty problem; they relocated to another city. Mission accomplished—grace received, but more importantly, grace given.

Rejection

Not all the people who require an extra helping of grace leave Agape with their lives changed. Barney and Becky drifted from a nearby church and started attending Agape. They were a young couple on the path to success. Barney worked at a car dealership and played bass with a local Christian band. Becky owned her own home-based business. Barney was recovering from back surgery and had an anger problem, partially due to his pain and the medication he was on. It wasn't long before they asked for prayer for their marriage problems. Jim and Jolene were happy to pray for them and even offered to meet with them for counseling. Things were going well until one weekend the marriage exploded over a small disagreement.

Barney gave up, immediately divorced Becky, and left for California. He took one of their three children with him, leaving Becky with the other two. With time they both remarried, and Becky drifted away from Agape. Sandell says, "We can offer God's grace and love to people, but there is no guarantee they will respond. These rejections hurt. The challenge is to keep them from making us hard toward new people the Lord brings our way."

Regardless of results, Agape continues to minister. "We are working on becoming what the Lord has called us to be, not what we think we should be. It is an ongoing challenge," Sandell says. "I want to see us live intentionally for Christ, every day, for the rest of our lives," Sandell continues. "It means we accept people who are unlovable, people who wouldn't find a church home anyplace else. It is extra work, and sometimes it is long hours." Why do they do it? Because God gives them the grace they require, and they pass it on to others, especially to those needing an extra helping.

Community

"Hey Jeremy, did you hear that Matt is starting a church?" "No, I didn't," Jeremy said. "Yeah," Nathan continued, "we're meeting in a room over at an apartment complex; do you think you could come?"

Jeremy liked Nathan and could tell he wanted him to come to his brother's church, so he agreed to come to a service—not because he thought it would interest him that much but as a favor to a friend. Jeremy hadn't found a church home yet and wasn't working real hard to find one. Occasionally he attended Harvest on Sunday nights, but most of the time homework or a football game trumped his spiritual obligation, and he just stayed home. After getting lost a couple of times trying to find the church, Jeremy found the "clubhouse" room—a small room with fifteen folding chairs, half of them empty. Not real impressive. But then again, Jeremy wasn't expecting much. He had heard Matt preach twice in chapel at Cal Baptist, and he was OK, and he knew several of the guys in the room, so he sat down with an open mind.

But there was no way he could anticipate what was about to happen. The service began rather laid back. "So how's your week going?" Matt asked. One at a time, each of the other nine people shared. So did Jeremy. "From that first service, I knew this was where I was supposed to be," Jeremy said. "God was going to do something amazing with this church, and I knew it."

What was so amazing? The preaching? The music? The art? The ambiance? No—Jeremy connected. He connected with the people. He connected with the mission. He connected with God. He saw community, and he wanted to be a part of it. Today Jeremy Crisp is Sandals's set-up team leader, in charge of fifty people who help prepare their rented facility for worship each week. But he is more than that; he is part of the body of Christ that is Sandals Church, Riverside—a place where he ministers and is ministered to.

Hanging Out

In April 1999, Jeremy went to the beach with some friends from church, just hanging out. As usually happens with most people, he mentioned something that was worrying him—he couldn't make his rent that month. After communion the next evening, the church had an open microphone for anyone who wanted to talk. Most of the people who spoke talked about what God was doing in their lives, but not Heather. Jeremy couldn't believe what she did, especially since he'd just met her the day before at the beach. "Jeremy can't make his rent this month," Heather said, "and I think we all should give him whatever we can spare to help out." Jeremy broke down and began weeping— not out of embarrassment but out of gratitude. "I've never had anybody do anything like that for me before," Jeremy said. After the service friends and strangers came by and pressed money into his hand. Not only was he able to make that month's rent, they gave him enough to pay the next month's and a DMV bill that was due.

That night he experienced community. Community isn't a group of people hanging out, and it isn't a program. Community is members of Christ's body rubbing souls with one another, entering into one another's pain, and celebrating one another's victories. Community is important to young adults. In his book *Intersecting Lives*, Geno Robinson writes that "they crave closeness. They desire to open themselves in relationships. They want real friendship and the freedom to share their deepest feelings."[1]

Jim Sandell says, "In community, we are better able to withstand trials." He illustrates his point by something he read in *Discover* magazine.[2] "If you take a sheet of paper and crumple it into as small a ball as you can, even if you are Mr. Universe, the ball is still 75 percent air. University of Chicago physicist Sidney Nagel wondered how air could hold up something as thin as a sheet of paper. Nagel and his colleagues investigated their question by crumpling Mylar sheets and placing them under a heavy piston. They found that though most of the compression took place in the first few seconds, the piston kept crushing the sheets by small amounts up to three weeks later."

Sandell continues, "The physicists discovered that squeezing a tightly crushed wad down to half its volume would take 64 times as such force as a normal person can exert. Nagel says, 'Even a weight lifter isn't 64 times stronger than the average person.' Paper balls resist compression because crumples in the paper consist of many small peaks joined by a network of ridges. To crush the ball further, each ridge has to buckle in two. Compressing the ball creates more ridges, which require even more energy to break."

"God's power is displayed as we form a network of ridges and small peaks that keep the community of believers from being crushed," Sandall concludes.

Authentic strengthening of community usually takes place in small groups organized around common interests, curiosities, and age. Churches organize their small groups differently. The Next Level Church in Denver organizes their small group ministry around their core values. The groups rotate in six-week intervals with three of the weeks focusing on teaching, one week on worship, one week on community, and one week on mission. The group leaders are autonomous, selecting their own teaching curriculum. Some follow popular books of the day; others take a book in the Bible and study it verse by verse; still others do topical studies. That's half of the cycle; the other half is spent on the church's other core values. One week they worship together; another, they just hang out or go on an outing; and the other is spent making a difference by doing a ministry in the community.

Vanguard Church in Colorado Springs, a church that meets in a movie theater, organizes their small groups using the motion picture rating system. X groups are for unbelievers exploring Christianity; R groups are recreational groups that meet in the summer. Growing groups, or G groups, are for believers and unbelievers. And PG groups are for progressively growing believers. The church requires group leaders to go through Team Player Connection training and have their material approved by Rick Clapp, executive pastor of network ministry, before they can teach in the small group ministry. The number one rule according to Clapp is "focus on the person before the information you want to give him. A leader shepherds them through life, not just giving them information."

"It's really gratifying to me when people begin to experience the power of the Word of God for themselves," says Adam Holz, a small group leader at Vanguard. "Whether it's an in-depth study of Romans or new believers looking at foundational passages such as John 3:16 for the first time, I'm always energized when people see how the Scriptures connect to their lives."

First Baptist Church of Fair Oaks, California, uses a traditional Sunday school structure to organize their small group ministry. Scott Worley was excited when a job transfer brought him back to Sacramento, his hometown. Worley was anxious to get closer to his parents and go back to his childhood church, First Baptist of Fair Oaks. His first Sunday back he and his wife Erica went to the young adult Sunday school department, ready to get involved again. Sitting across from him were Bill and Mari Worley—his dad and stepmom. Not cool. It isn't that they didn't love their parents and want to spend time with them; it was that they wanted to be around people their own age. Instead of looking for another church, Scott and Erica worked with some other young adults ranging in age from twenty-one to twenty-six to reach the generation that was missing from their church. Today it is a vibrant, growing part of First Baptist.

One of the principles they've used to reach their generation is to plan monthly gatherings where the small group can just hang out together. The events don't always come off as planned, but somehow the dynamics of community usually emerge. On one occasion the group planned to go camping at Fallen Leaf Lake, near Lake Tahoe. Everyone showed up, and so did the torrential rains. "To this day," says Jim Laing, a member of the small group, "the people who went have a strong bond." Everyone had to pitch in to help everybody else pack up and go home. The experience, even though it was unpleasant, brought the group together. "Our primary purpose is evangelism," Laing says. "Our primary method is relationships, and our primary activity is Bible study." Their goal isn't forming relationships. Their goal is to bring people into a relationship with Jesus Christ, but the method they use to accomplish that goal is building relationships.

According to senior pastor J. T. Reed, the key to the church's growth is the young adults' emphasis on building relationships. "Two or three of our groups have really caught on to the relationship principle, and it is contributing to the growth in our young adult area." Worley sums it up when he says, "This group just likes being together."

"People are not looking for a friendly church," says Josh Hunt, author of *You Can Double Your Sunday School in Two Years or Less*, "they are looking for friends."[3] Churches stop growing when they stop being friends with new people and settle with being friendly.

Alive and Breathing

Organization is important, but community doesn't exist until the small group becomes an organism—a living, breathing organism that is the body of Christ. It can't just be a collection of people of the same age and interests; it has to be more. Being in community, as a part of the body of Christ, means we radically follow Christ's commands as we care for one another.

"I hate the words *authentic, real,* and *community,*" says Mark Driscoll, pastor of Mars Hill Fellowship in Seattle. "They are a mantra that has been pounded [into our heads] that means nothing." [For some people] community means we get a group like us and complain about everything. We sit around deconstructing and don't do anything. There is a difference between being real and being critical." Community isn't criticizing people outside the clique and not confronting one another. "Community isn't listening without judging. It is speaking the truth to one another," Driscoll continues. "It isn't based upon all being alike. It isn't because we all play the guitar or have a goatee." In his book *Being the Body,* Charles Colson writes, "Just as we cannot do justice to September 11, we could not begin to detail all the ways that churches across our nation lived their faith in its wake. In the darkest hour, so many of the people of God stood as His church, doing what the church does best: being the community that brings hope and comfort to brokenness and pain."[4] Community, at its core, is more than hanging out with pals or fitting in with a group. It is more than a program or an organization. It exists, in its purest form, when the church is mystically transformed into the body of Christ. Nathan Brown, administrative pastor at Sandals, Riverside, experienced this on August 21, 2000. Nathan wanted everything to be just right for Danielle's birthday. It took some planning to pull it off, but logistics is Nathan's thing. After all, if he can relocate across town a congregation averaging eight hundred in worship, he could pull off a surprise party for his wife. It was no big deal. They dropped Leah, their newborn daughter, off at Heather and Carlos's and headed out to a steak house for the evening. Instead of going straight to pick up their daughter after dinner, Nathan made up an excuse of needing to pick up some chairs in order to stop by his brother's house. As he looked out of the corner of his eye at his wife, Nathan knew he'd pulled it off. She didn't suspect a thing.

Nathan pulled into Matt's driveway. Everything was normal. The crowd had done a great job hiding their cars. "You wanna come in for a minute and say hi to Matt and Tammy while I go get the chairs?" Nathan asked. He opened Danielle's door, and they walked hand in hand to the front door.

"Surprise!" Everyone yelled. Danielle was beaming. Usually she doesn't like attention drawn to herself, but she seemed to be soaking in the moment. The room was filled with church leaders from Sandals, but they were more than that—they were friends, they were family.

Nathan had worked hard to help his brother Matt build Sandals, Riverside. They are an unusual pair. Matt is a people person, a frontline leader. His personality is dynamic. There is something about him that makes people want to buy in to his dream and follow him. Matt is a dreamer. Not Nathan. His feet are firmly planted on the ground. His attitude is, "Tell me the dream, and with God's help, I'll make it happen." He's all about making stuff happen. Little did he know that the church he'd helped his brother build would become such an important community for his family. And I'm not talking about what was happening at Danielle's surprise party either. That kind of community is easy. Anyone can throw bean dip on a table, invite some friends over, and call it a party. But what was about to happen wasn't so elementary. It can't be explained by leadership, dreams, or administration. It was a God thing.

The room was immaculately decorated. There were tons of presents and food everywhere. As Danielle and Nathan were going around greeting everyone and thanking them for the party, a wrought iron gate slammed shut. Leah, Nathan and Danielle's daughter, jerked. A few seconds later, Carlos noticed that she clinched her fist, pulled her elbows into her side, then stretched them out. Carlos immediately called for Danielle, "Hey Danielle, Leah's upset. Can you calm her down?" When Danielle retrieved her six-week-old baby, she could tell that something was wrong. She grabbed a lock of Danielle's hair and started yanking on it and began shuddering. Nathan glanced over at Danielle and saw sheer terror in her eyes. He took Leah from her and tried to take Danielle's hair out of Leah's hands. Leah made a deep guttural sound—the sound of the last bit of air leaving her tiny lungs. It wasn't an "I need attention" cry or an "I'm hurt" cry. It was far beyond those familiar sounds.

Leah was dying. Nathan walked into the house. Leah was turning blue. He walked away from the florescent lights, hoping the strange coloring was a result of the lighting.

When he entered a room with incandescent lights, Leah's color had changed again: this time she was gray. There were three people in the room: Matt's in-laws and nineteen-year-old Elissa. Nathan started CPR and told Elissa to grab the keys in the baby bag and to come with him. Nathan made a split-second decision to drive the four miles to the hospital himself, instead of dialing 911. Danielle burst through the front door and ran out to the front driveway just in time to see Nathan speeding down the street.

Danielle collapsed into a rubbery heap. Matt walked up behind her and helped her to her feet. Matt drove Danielle to the hospital. Inside, the party turned into a prayer meeting.

Nathan drove. Elissa breathed into Leah's cold lips. Nathan performed chest compressions and sped as quickly as he could to the emergency room, running four red lights in the process. He didn't bother parking the car. He pulled into the ambulance's parking place, put on the emergency brake, took Leah from Elissa and ran into the hospital.

"My baby's not breathing." Immediately, the doors to the emergency room flew open. A nurse showed Nathan where to take his baby as another nurse set off the Code Blue. As Nathan handed Leah over to the nurse, he knew his baby was dead. Eight doctors and countless nurses scrambled to Leah's bedside and began working on her. Another nurse took Nathan in a room where he could be alone. He could still hear Elissa's words to Leah in the car: "Hold on baby, you can do it, hold on." The events of the past few minutes swirled through his head. In the car Leah seemed to respond as Elissa performed CPR, but Nathan didn't know if that was because she was breathing or because air was being forced into her. Nathan reached for his cell phone and called Danielle's twin sister in New York, his mom and dad, and Pastor Tom Lance, his sponsoring church pastor, to tell them what was going on and to ask for their prayers.

Then things got quiet—real quiet. Too quiet. Nathan's hands began to shake. His body jittered. His muscles tensed.

As he assessed the situation, the lead doctor looked at everybody and said, "We need to pray." They defibulated her five times, incubated her, and did everything they could to save her.

"Excuse me, Mr. Brown. Would you mind moving your car and parking it in the parking lot?" At the moment the last thing Nathan was worried about was his car, but grudgingly he did as the voice requested. As Nathan walked back toward the hospital, Matt's car pulled in. He called to Danielle. They came over. "What's going on?" Matt asked. Nathan didn't answer. He just held on to his wife. "It's not good, is it?" Danielle asked. Nathan responded, "She was never ours." Inside, Danielle held Nathan tight and sobbed. A nurse came over and asked if they'd like to move over to the meditation room. *I know what's happening,* Nathan thought, *they're separating us from the general population so we don't scare the others when the doctor comes out with the bad news.*

Inside the room others from the church joined Nathan, Danielle, Elissa, and Matt, and they prayed. "Lord, no matter what happens, we'll serve you," Nathan prayed. "There's no doubt in my mind that you can heal her, but whichever way it goes, we'll serve you." Others prayed. They prayed for healing and comfort. The prayer circle ended with someone saying, "In the name of Jesus we pray that she'll be healed. Amen."

As they looked up, a doctor rushed into the room and said, "We got her back!" Leah wasn't out of the woods, but she was alive. The doctors transferred her to a larger hospital. Nathan and Danielle were in no condition to drive, so people from the church drove them. The next morning they finally crashed around one o'clock at the hospital, but they weren't alone. Two men from the church stayed behind and prayed over them all night long.

The next night some other men stayed and prayed over them. Sandals people brought meals for the family; one family parked their RV on the hospital parking lot so the Browns would have a place to stay. Up to thirty people a night stopped by to pray. People cleaned their house for them and did their laundry so they'd have clean clothes. Some of the people at the party began fasting that night and spent the next two weeks in prayer and fasting for Leah. One night, about eleven, Nathan had to sign a release authorizing an emergency surgery. He picked up his cell phone and called Tony, the community pastor, and Mark, the prayer minister, and asked them to wake up all the small group leaders and have them call their small groups and ask them to pray for Leah. That night the church rose up in prayer for one who could not pray for herself. Some of them drove to the hospital and prayer-walked around the building. And God heard their prayers.

Many of these people who surrounded the Browns were single without kids, but all were drawn into the circle of community with compassion for Leah. It wasn't that they fit a demographic profile or that they had that much in common with Nathan, Danielle, and Leah. It was that the love of Christ compelled them to minister and connect with a brother and sister in Christ.

It isn't what people said that meant a lot to the Browns; it is what they *did* that counted most. "The people who were the most awesome were the quiet people who were just there," Nathan says. "The people who said 'I love you' and stood with us so we didn't have to be alone. Those were the people who had the most impact on us during our trial."

Today Leah is OK. She's met all her developmental goals for her age, and Nathan and Danielle are optimistic—optimistic about their daughter's future and their church's.

Some people settle for picnics on the Fourth of July or potluck dinners after church and think they are experiencing Christian fellowship. But in the "valley of the shadow of death," others find real community. Sometimes the shadow is theirs, and sometimes it is someone else's. Regardless, they learn that in those times God is there, in the midst of his people in community.

Technology

Remember the Y2K crisis? When all was said and done, Y2K turned out to be Y2YAWN! No real problems. Yet

some people listened to the prophets of doom and radically altered their lives. A man I knew in New Mexico was so convinced that mayhem would follow Y2K that he sold out and moved to a remote location. He stockpiled food, installed a water tank, and in effect checked out of society to avoid the potential problems of a technological shutdown. He and his wife were preparing for the worst, and the worst did happen for him. In late December 1999, he died from complications resulting from a stroke. Instead of enjoying his children and grandchildren, he spent the last days of his life preparing for what he wouldn't live to see. Now his widow is left in the middle of nowhere, and I'm left wondering what she will do.

Is technology isolating people from one another the same way the threat of a technological meltdown isolated this man from his family? It's easy this side of the twenty-first century to second-guess this man's wisdom in stockpiling supplies and checking out of society. He could have been right, and then I would be the one looking foolish today. That's the problem with the future. None of us really knows what it holds. Our tendency is to feel a degree of certainty about the past and fearfulness of the future. Perhaps that's why there are more historians than futurists.

Half Empty or Half Full?

What do you see when you gaze into the future? Do the patterns you see in our society make you optimistic? Or would you just as soon go back to the twentieth century? Are there some indicators that concern you? Could there be a Y2K crisis yet? Those warning us of a possible Y2K computer glitch stressed the possibility of an acute crisis but ignored a chronic problem that has been developing for years.

What words would you use to describe the era we're in? The most common word I hear is *postmodern*. Personally, I don't like the term. It tells what the era follows, but it doesn't describe what the era *is*. Terms like *Dark Ages* or *Enlightenment* communicate. They are rich and descriptive, something *postmodern* lacks. That word has a trendy feel to me, but I doubt it will linger in our vocabulary for long. And really, that's the point. Nobody really knows what is ahead, but we do know what is behind. We've left the modern age. Since nobody really knows what to call this age, we simply call it postmodern.

At the end of the modern era, mankind was wrestling with who God is and even questioned his existence. In the 1880s Nietzsche declared that "God is dead," and before the turn of the twentieth century, George Bernard Shaw and H. G. Wells chimed in saying the twentieth century would mark the end of the world's "religious phase." Yet today a church meets in Russia's Museum of Religion and Atheism—the former center of atheism. Nearly half of the United States population regularly attends worship, while revival is sweeping through Latin America, and Christianity grows behind China's iron curtain.[5] Nietzsche, Shaw, and Wells have long since decayed in their graves, and God continues to live! God is alive and well, and Americans know it. According to a 1999 Barna survey, only 7 percent of Americans view themselves as atheists or agnostics.[6]

The debate does not center on God as much as it used to. Now people are asking, What is human life? In a *Reader's Digest* article, J. Alex Tarquinio raises an interesting question: "Behind lab doors, scientists are working to end aging, disease, and pain. But are we changing what it means to be human?"[7] Over time there has been a subtle dehumanizing of mankind. James Parker, professor of worldview and culture at Southern Baptist Theological Seminary in Louisville, Kentucky, calls this era a "posthuman" age.

People are asking if we are just another species of animal or if there is something special about the human race. The Christian worldview has an answer rooted in Genesis 1:27: "And God created man in His own image, in the image of God He created him; male and female He created them" (NASB). Christians affirm that we did not evolve from animals but that God created us. He created us in his own image. We are special because we are image bearers of God.

That is the Christian worldview, but it is a minority view.

In 1985, Simon & Schuster published Phil Donahue's book *The Human Animal*. It is out of print today, but the message of its title is still in vogue: humans are just another animal—nothing special or unique about us. Have science and technology contributed to dehumanization? Advancements in science have led everyone to ponder the question, What is human, anyway? Are cyborgs human? Cyborgs are partially human and partially machines. They are partially born and partially made.

What if medical science could cure a certain type of deafness with cochlear implants? Would that be acceptable? According to Jack Wheeler, CEO of the Deafness Research Foundation, this device "could conquer newborn deafness in America."[8]

Should doctors implant pacemakers to help regulate irregular hearts? What about an artificial heart? What about an artificial, programmable brain?

Why is that a line we're not willing to cross?

What about cloning? Currently researchers are toying with using this technology to bring back extinct species. In an October 8, 2000, article, the Associated Press reports that a cow in Sioux City, Iowa, is pregnant with a rare Asian gaur fetus. Scientists took the egg of the cow, stripped it of its DNA, and fused the egg with a skin cell from a gaur. In effect, they've created an embryo the cow's uterus will accept that is genetically a gaur. Technically, "Noah," the name of the fetus, has no father; it was artificially induced to begin dividing and growing. Should scientists use cloning to preserve a species? Or to bring a species back to life? What about humans? Should there be human cloning?

Why is that a line we're not willing to cross?

What about fetuses? Are unborn babies human? When I think about the Girl Scouts, I think about thin mint cookies. I've always thought the organization was one that taught traditional values to girls. But did you know that the Senior Girl Scout Handbook for ages 14–17 talks about how girls can end pregnancy and advocates euthanasia under some circumstances?[9] Has abortion become so accepted in our day that the Girl Scouts organization feels responsible to inform girls about it? A few years ago I wrote an antiabortion devotional and sent it out over my e-mail list, FreshStart Devotionals. Promptly, one irate reader responded by asking me to take her e-mail address off the list. The reason she gave was that I shouldn't mix religion and politics. My question is, When did abortion become a political issue and cease being a religious one?

Now some people want to use undeveloped embryos for medical research. Recently, Michael J. Fox testified before Congress about the promise of stem cell research for Parkinson's, the disease he suffers from. Stem cells have the potential of becoming any kind of human cell. Researchers believe that using these cells could help them find a cure for diseases like Parkinson's and diabetes. According to *ABC News*, "Fox urged people not to have a 'knee-jerk' response to the stem cell debate and said the research had the potential to 'literally change the world.'"[10]

I like Michael J. Fox, and I was sad when I heard he had Parkinson's disease. When I heard his plea for stem cell research, I wanted to do whatever it takes to help him with his problem. But I'm still left asking, Should embryos be used for research? What about aborted fetuses? Would this research create a demand for them on the open market resulting in planned abortions?

So what is the Christian response to the threats of the third millennium? Should we do battle with science? Do we organize political opposition? No, we did that in the modern age, and all it did was alienate us from culture. Then what do we do? Instead of cursing the darkness, why don't we do what Jesus told us to do and shine a light? At a Summit for the Third Millennium, hosted by LifeWay Christian Resources at Glorieta Conference Center in New Mexico, Dallas Willard, professor of philosophy at the University of Southern California, quoted the Great Commission and said, "If you want to know what to do while we deal with the reality of the coming millennium, this is it!" Since Jesus promised he would be with us to the end of the age, we can rest assured that he will be with the church in the third millennium if we will let the gospel shine. And if we will let the gospel light shine, Jesus promises that those who see our "good works will glorify our Father who is in heaven." Isn't that our goal?

The future of the church isn't shuddering in a corner, fearful of what's coming next or fighting in political arenas. It is letting the light shine on the human condition. Jesus said, "You are the light of the world. A city set on a hill cannot be hidden. Nor do men light a lamp, and put it under the peck measure, but on the lampstand; and it gives light to all who are in the house. Let your light shine before men in such a way that they may see your good works, and glorify your Father who is in heaven" (Matt. 5:14–16 NASB).

Yes, there is plenty of darkness in the world, but that is why light is needed.

Human Again

What does it mean to be human? Does it mean we are destined to sin? Or does it mean we have the potential to commune with God? The gospel restores humanity—the ability to commune with God. When Jesus said, "Neither do I condemn you" to the woman caught in the act of adultery, he restored her dignity. When he said, "Go and sin no more," he restored her humanity. She wasn't trapped in her pattern of animalistic behavior anymore. Jesus gave her the potential to break those patterns and begin again. He set her free to fulfill her potential. The gospel can restore the humanity of those who have a hole in their soul because of the impact of the isolation and dehumanization of technology. A high-tech world needs a high-touch church. A church can be the context for fellowship and restored humanity, one person at a time.

Human touch is powerful. As part of treatment for thyroid cancer, I drank radioactive iodine to kill any cancer cells surgery didn't get. The procedure was physically painless but emotionally devastating. Because I was radioactive after drinking the medicine, I was quarantined for two days but in isolation from my family for one week. I was untouchable—literally. My doctor spoke to me from the door behind a lead barrier; the nurses wore protective suits when they walked into the room. My family and friends were prohibited from visiting me. A week later, for the first time after the treatment, my wife gave me a big hug as I left for work. I felt human again.

I wonder how the leper felt when Jesus reached out his hand and touched him?

www.thefuturechurch.com

Conclusion
The Lighthouse

*E*arly into my research, I became aware that the Future Church is not a model to be duplicated, and I didn't have any desire to make the church I served into a carbon copy of any church I visited. In an interview with *Leadership Journal*, Mark Driscoll says, "Our temptation is always to take an approach and turn that into a system, and I think that's the death of what the Spirit of God is trying to do."[1] I worked hard to resist that temptation. Don't get me wrong; I picked up some great ideas from the churches I visited. I liked the welcome packet the greeters at The Next Level Church in Denver gave me. It was in a bright red oversized envelope that made it easy for church leaders to identify me as a visitor, and it was filled with helpful information. I also liked the way Graceland in Santa Cruz laid out their services. Instead of music, preaching, go home, they wove teaching and worship throughout the service. And I loved the simplicity of Mars Hill Fellowship's PowerPoint presentations. They use a black background with a white Courier font. We do all of those things now.

But really, methodology isn't the issue. Each congregation is different in style and methodology, and God's Spirit is shaping them into what he wants them to be. "[Contemporary churches] tend to place a great deal of emphasis on methodology and management," says Ron Johnson, pastor of Pathways Church in Denver, "but they typically are not very thoughtful about how to read culture or the human soul. This is where the Future Church is making a break with the past. The Future Church will be communities of faith that will help people read the soul and the culture and will model reading the Bible, not as a manual but as a means of grace for communion with God." That's the kind of church I wanted to lead, not one that focused on methodology but one focused on the soul and on God's will.

Our transformation began with a passion in my heart— a passion to reach young adults. I spoke publicly about it and the opportunity we had to be world changers if we would. We prayed that we would become a lighthouse, a church that warns society of dangers and points people into a safe harbor.

After interviewing several pastors, I concluded that we would never reach people we don't value. It would be easy to say that Westwinds and Mosaic reach artists because they value art and that Agape reaches EGR (extra grace required) people because they value grace. There is some truth to that. But there is a deeper truth. Westwinds and Mosaic do more than value art; they value artists. That's why they reach artists. Agape does more than value grace; they value people who require extra grace. That's why they reach EGR people. Parkview reaches homeless people because they value them and treat them with dignity. Valuing people means that we value the things that they value.

One Sunday evening I said to the handful of people that gathered, "Why don't we turn this service over to the young people in our church and let them plan the worship service? We may not like all the music they pick out, but that will be OK; it would be nice to see them involved, wouldn't it?" They agreed, and we began transitioning the church into the twenty-first century, beginning with the evening service.

At the same time we were remodeling an educational wing of the building into a multipurpose area with accordion walls to provide fellowship space. So we remodeled it in such a way that we could move our evening service into the space when it was completed. Instead of buying rectangular tables and folding chairs, we ordered round tables and chairs with padded seating. We put in a screen and projector to run PowerPoint and purchased an electronic drum set and keyboard for the new band that was forming. We put individual speakers in zones throughout the room so we could have part of the room quieter than other parts of the room for our senior citizens who prefer their music quieter.

The youth introduced the church to music I'd never heard. "Delirious," "Sonic Flood," and "Third Day" have become the staples of the service. But they also choose from the great hymns of the faith. Some of the worshippers sit in rows of chairs we place right in front of the band, but most of them sit at round tables spread throughout the room. We dim the lights and put candles on the tables to add ambiance. The service begins with a set of music, transitions into a teaching time, and then ends with a longer set of worship. The worship time prepares the people's hearts for the teaching, and then the teaching prepares their hearts for worship.

Sometimes we have "table talk," a time for the people to discuss a Bible passage or current issue; other times we have a protracted time of prayer instead of a long teaching time. The people are responding to this service. One day we may have to move back into the auditorium because there have been some weeks when there wasn't enough room for everyone to sit down.

Brutal Honesty

"Hello, my name is Jennifer, and I'm stationed out at DLI. I'm going to be here for about nine months and am looking for a church. Do you have anything for single young adults at your church?" "No, we don't," I said. "We have several married couples from DLI who have come and are plugged into the church, but the single young adults don't seem to stick. But that's not what we want. We have a heart to reach them, but we need help to do it. Will you come and help us?"

As the phone call continued, I told Jennifer that we were praying that we could reach the students at DLI, married and single alike, and I told her about the changes we were making. For one, we were trying to knock down age barriers to ministry. We not only involve young adults in ministry; we include teenagers too. Future Churches don't view teenagers as the church of the future; they understand that teens are the church of today. We've shifted from ministering *to* teenagers to ministering *with* teenagers. A fifteen-year-old runs our sound system on Sunday mornings; our evening band is comprised primarily of teenagers with some young adults. A nineteen-year-old is giving our announcements on Sunday mornings, and a fourteen-year-old is on the nursery committee.

I told Jennifer that if she came to our church, she could be a part of the church, not just of a department of the church. And I told her about Encounter.

Close Encounter

We moved our midweek service to Thursdays because DLI students don't have physical training on Thursdays, making it one of the easier days of the week for them. But that wasn't the only shift we made. Instead of having a pastor-led Bible study, we went to a small group ministry. Our classes are designed to help make a difference in the lives of those who can make a difference in the world. In effect, it is a lay seminary or discipleship training on steroids.

Jennifer's phone call came a week before Encounter's launch. At the time we had no idea how Encounter would change the landscape of our church or that it would become a primary tool we'd use to prepare people to be world changers. Knowing that it would be difficult for families to eat before coming and that a home-cooked meal would be a treat for soldiers used to eating in a mess hall, our hospitality committee decided to provide a hot meal before the small group meetings. We gather for fellowship and a meal at 5:45 and meet in our classes from 6:30 to 8:00.

Today Encounter averages more on Thursday nights than we did on Sunday mornings when I first came to the church, and it is certainly more than the handful that attended our pastor-led Wednesday night services. The whole idea took some getting used to for a church that traditionally has a midweek service on Wednesday. Remember, this church is sixty years old. Changes don't always come easily for an established church. But to the credit of our people, they didn't let tradition get in the way of effective ministry.

But really, some of the changes we've made were easy. They took very little effort on the part of the church body. The easiest thing to change, I've found, is myself. It was relatively easy for me to learn to preach narrative sermons. I don't exclusively preach narrative sermons, but even when I don't, I try to buttress a topical or expository sermon with elements of the narrative sermon. Rarely do I preach propositional messages or preach from the "expert" vantage point. Instead, I preach as a peer, a fellow pilgrim on a faith walk.

The day I relinquished the pulpit at announcement time was an easy change for the congregation to handle. Not only did it free me from having to remember everything people wanted me to say, but it also allowed me to make a statement to the congregation while sitting in my seat without opening my mouth. First it says I'm not the epicenter of the church's activities, and second it says something about whom we value. We show whom we value by whom we put on the stage, so when I turned the announcement duties over to a young female, I was making a statement: we value young adults, and we value females.

It was easy for the congregation to use some of our worship time in contrition and repentance and not just to focus on celebration. Celebration will always get the lion's share of the time, but it doesn't have to get all of the time. One of the most powerful Sunday morning services we've had included a ten-minute segment of silent prayer, supported only by instrumental music. I'd read Psalm 51 and encouraged the congregation to confess their sins before a holy God before we went into the prayer time. We broke the silent prayer with a public prayer of contrition, followed by our youth band singing "Breathe," a song that affirms that we are desperate for God.

It wasn't hard for the church to accept the use of some art in our worship services. One Easter Sunday, we displayed art on the big screen that corresponded with the music and the teaching. Routinely, I use art in our PowerPoint worship slides. But we do more than just project art on a screen. An artist in the church painted a beautiful painting that now hangs in the foyer of the church. It captures our mission— to point people home to heaven. Immediately after the September 11 terrorist attacks, I asked our children to paint some pictures on butcher paper to encourage the congregation. At the end of the service, they brought their paintings to the front to show the congregation what they were working on. They brought up two beautiful American flags that we displayed in our foyer as a symbol of our children's hope.

Our Only Constant

But not all changes are easy. Because we reach military personnel who will be with us only from six months to eighteen months, our ministry is cyclical. Over the past few years we've had times when we've had to bring in chairs for worship and convert storerooms into classrooms because we were reaching so many people. But the pendulum swings both ways. On one Sunday in June 2002, we said good-bye to over forty people who were moving to their next duty station. During that year we lost 150 people who moved away, a number just shy of our average attendance for the year. We've had times when we were able to pay extra money against our debt and other times when we had to watch every dime we spent. Whether our attendance is up or down, we pursue our mission.

Our mission itself makes our congregation fluid. We are "making disciples" of people whom we will give back to churches around the world. We have alumni scattered around the world, taking a passion for ministry with them as they go. We know that if we focus on reaching, loving, nurturing, and equipping people who will only be here a short time, we can have a great kingdom impact, but we also know that it will contribute to the instability of a church in constant flux. We continue to minister with the conviction that it is the place God gave us to stand and that from here we will move the world.

Not only are we going into the world; the world is coming to us. A population shift is occurring in Seaside, the community where our church is located, from predominantly Anglo and African-American to Hispanic. We could ignore that shift and focus solely on the military community, but to do so would have long-term consequences for the health of our church. It takes a strong civilian contingency in the church to be able to facilitate a ministry to the military population. Seaside is part of the world we are working to change; we must reach them too. But how?

Ever since I was a child, I've had a heart for missions and have been willing to go overseas if God calls me. Certainly my wife knew about my heart for missions and that I'd go if God calls me. But what she didn't know was that I'd been praying he would open that door and that he'd lay it on her heart to want to go too. I prayed that if God gives me the desire, he would give it to her too—not just to go with me because I was going but also to go because God was moving her to go. We never talked about it. Not once did I ask her how she felt about going overseas. I just prayed and asked God to speak to her. During the summer of 2002 it happened. Susan initiated the conversation and said the words I'd longed to hear: "I believe God may be calling us to missions, and if he does, I'm willing to go." I didn't tell her about my prayer at that time; instead, we just held each other and wept.

Later I went on a "praise walk"—just me and God. "Thank you, God, for speaking to Susan," I said. "You are an awesome and powerful God. Our answer is yes. You point the direction and we'll go. We're ready." I'm not sure what I expected God to say in the silence that followed, but certainly not what he said. "I'm glad you're willing to go and be a missionary," I sensed God saying. "Too bad you're not willing to be a missionary right where I've put you." Ouch!

I immediately thought of the last thing Mark Driscoll, pastor of Mars Hill Fellowship in Seattle, said to me when I interviewed him: "Think like a missionary, and do what works in your area." Being a missionary doesn't have to do with geographic location as much as with point of view. I knew exactly what I needed to do. I needed to think like a missionary. If I were a missionary assigned to Seaside, California, one of the first things I would do is learn the language of the people. So I went back to college to take Spanish. I've finished my first year now and have some basic skills, but I'm still a long way from being able to preach in Spanish. But that doesn't mean we couldn't get started. Joel Jimenez, pastor of Emmanuel Baptist Church in Salinas, agreed to come help us launch Spanish services in our auditorium on Thursday evenings, while Encounter is in session throughout the rest of the building. Before the sessions we eat together and encourage cross-cultural fellowship around the table. Pastor Joel preaches, and I say a few words or give a prayer. The worship service is in its infancy stage now, but it is showing signs of life. We are beginning to reach people from the community. Our goal is not necessarily to begin a new church, though we know that could happen. We just don't want to lose a passion for the community while we work to move the world, even if it means we have to deal with more change.

Intentional Dissatisfaction

For the most part things are going well at Lighthouse, but I don't want to give the impression that everybody likes everything that is going on at our church. In fact, if they did, I'd think something was wrong. We are a multigenerational, multiethnic, multicultural church. I often say, "If you like everything that is going on in this church, you're not paying attention." After it gets real quiet, I continue, "Not every service and every ministry we do was designed with your generation in mind. Some of it was planned for the person who sits next to you."

I suppose we could major on conformity instead of diversity and target a specific demographic group for our services. And we could just reach the old or the young and let the others find another place to go. We could offer services in only one language, even though the population has shifted in our area. Instead, we've chosen to accept a certain level of dissatisfaction, knowing that no one generation or culture in the church will always get their way. And because we do, I watch with great joy every week when the people gather. I watch the old hug the young and the singles play with other people's children. I overhear a middle-aged woman explain to a new mother how to treat diaper rash, or one of the local men telling a young father where he can get the best deal on tires for his car. Then someone walks up to introduce a new friend they've brought.

"I want you to meet our pastor," they'll say. As I extend my hand to meet their friends, I'll say, "Welcome to our church. I know you're going to like it here." I don't say that because they'll like everything we do. I say that because I know they'll like who we are—a church that is passionately pursuing our mission to move the world.

And I know that as long as we stay on that journey, we are a church with a bright future—a Future Church.

Afterword

When they lived in New York City, the Turners went to Broadway plays whenever they could fit them into their busy schedules, but their real passion was attending off-Broadway productions of Shakespeare. These productions are an acquired taste but one the Turners had acquired. Some of the actors were getting their start in such productions. Others were finishing out careers that never really took off. But it was New York, and the plays were done with excellence.

The Turners always made an event out of their theater evenings. Dressed in their finest clothes, they'd travel by limousine to their favorite restaurant and to the theater. They did more than enjoy their evenings out—they savored them.

When the clock struck retirement age, they sold their apartment in the city and bought a country house in upstate New York. They loved the tranquility and the slower pace, but they missed their theater. In the early part of their retirement, they would take excursion trips into the city just to go to the theater. But as they got older, they didn't have the health to travel, so they settled into their recliners for whatever entertainment they could muster up with their remote control. One afternoon he saw a story in the weekly newspaper about a high school production of *Macbeth*. He asked his wife if she'd like to go. Of course, she jumped at the opportunity.

On the way home, she broke the silence by saying, "Well, it sure wasn't like it was in the city." "No, you're right," he replied. After a long pause, he interjected, "But it was Shakespeare."

The church isn't anywhere near perfect. None of these churches I've written about in this book is perfect, and neither is yours. Our churches are filled with flawed people, but it is the body of Christ, a place where imperfect people like me and you can stand beside one another before a God who is worthy of our worship and connect with him and with one another.

Acknowledgments

This book would have been impossible without the cooperation of church leaders across the country who allowed me to interview them and analyze their worship services, and who then proofread the chapters where they were quoted to ensure accuracy. I thank them all for what they taught me about ministry.

Thank you to Gregory C. Benoit and to James F. Couch Jr. for helping me communicate my message in this form. You've vastly improved my original manuscript. Thank you.

Thank you to Leonard Goss and the people at Broadman & Holman and to James F. Couch and the people at Serendipity House who worked together in a model of Christian cooperation to introduce this book to its current audience.

And thank you to Susan, Stephen, and Jamie Wilson for allowing me to drag them around the country during our family vacations to see what God is doing in his churches. You never complained once. Thank you.

Some of the contents of this book were published in other forms before inclusion in this book. Portions first appeared in *Transformations*, *Fresh Illustrations*, and other periodicals. My thanks to the editors of *Leadership Journal*, Baptist Press, *California Southern Baptist*, *Growing Churches*, *Rev*, and *Your Church* for the way their work improved mine.

Also, thank you to Anita Harriger, Esther Greenwalt, and Susan Jones, who read early editions of the manuscript and gave me constructive criticism.

Finally, thank you to Dr. Tom Stringfellow and Parakaleo Ministries for underwriting the expenses of my research.

Notes

Fulcrum Point 1: Get Creative

1. http://www.csulb.edu/~jvancamp/doc28.html/.

2. Jacques Barzun, *From Dawn to Decadence* (New York: HarperCollins, 2000), 139.

3. Randall Balmer, "The Kincade Crusade," *Christianity Today*, December 4, 2000. http://www.christianitytoday.com/ct/2000/014/6.48.html/.

4. Lee Strobel, *God's Outrageous Claims* (Grand Rapids: Zondervan, 1998), 170.

Fulcrum Point 2: Get Spiritual

1. Dan Kimball, *The Emerging Church: Vintage Christianity for New Generations* (Grand Rapids: Zondervan, 2003), 83.

2. *Monterey County Herald*, religion section, 25 May 2002.

3. Barna 2000/2001 Conference, San Jose, CA, 6 November 2000.

4. Ron Martoia, *Moph: The Texture of Leadership for Tomorrow's Church* (Loveland, CO: Group Publishing, 2002), 135.

5. Dan Kimball, "Holy Man or Business Man?" *Rev.*, January/February 2002, 78.

Fulcrum Point 3: Get Radical

1. Kenneth Woodward, "The Changing Face of the Church," *Newsweek*, 16 April 2001, 16.

2. Barna 2000/2001 Conference, San Jose, CA, 6 November 2000.

Fulcrum Point 4: Get Real

1. *Virginia Baptists' Weekly*, 11 October 2001, 1.

2. *Newsweek*, 30 June 2003, 21.

3. *Beckett's Baseball Card Monthly*, July 1999, 6.

4. Larry Crabb, *The Safest Place on Earth* (Nashville: Word, 1999), 115.

5. Alan Simpson, *Reader's Digest*, March 2001, 61.

6. *USA Today*, 16 June 2003, 13A.

7. http://www.pastors.com/MT/4/?id=4&artid=151& expand=1/.

8. Frank Lewis, "Preaching That Restores," *Leadership Journal*, Winter 2001, 40.

9. *Washington Times*, 13 March 2001.

Fulcrum Point 5: Get Truthful

1. *California Southern Baptist*, January 2002, 15.

2. http://www.barna.org/cgi-bin/PageCategory.asp? CategoryID=37/.

3. *Religion Today,* 7 March 2000.

4. William Watkins, *The New Absolutes* (Minneapolis: Bethany House, 1997), 26.

5. http://216.87.179.136/cgi_bin/PageCategory.asp? Categoryid=39/.

6. http://www.cnn.com/transcripts/0007/06/lkl.00.html/.

7. *On Mission,* February 2002, 14–15.

8. William Barclay, *The Acts of the Apostles* (Great Britain: Westminster), 141.

9. *Newsweek,* 20 July 2002, 64.

Fulcrum Point 6: Get Multi

1. Geno Robinson, "Intersecting Lives," *California Southern Baptist,* January 1998, 13.

2. Dan Kimball, *The Emerging Church: Vintage Christianity for New Generations* (Grand Rapids: Zondervan, 2003), 33.

3. http://www.cnn.com/2002/TECH/internet/02/26 /auction.fraud.vigilantes.idg/index.html/.

4. "Schechem," in *Zondervan Pictorial Encyclopedia of the Bible* (Grand Rapids: Zondervan, 1975).

5. http://www.sltrib.com/09022000/saturday/18525.htm/

6. Associated Press, New York, 16 June 1998, 9:22 EDT.

7. http://www.skeptictank.org/hs/lott_gay.htm/.

8. Tony Carnes, "Design Interference," *Christianity Today,* December 4, 2000, http:///www.christianitytoday. com/ct/ 2000/014/18.20.htmo./.www.foxnews.com, 1 January 2001.

Fulcrum Point 7: Get Connected

1. Geno Robinson, "Intersecting Lives," *California Southern Baptist*, January 1998, 46.

2. "The Incredible Power of Crumpled Paper," *Discover*, August 2002, 13.

3. Josh Hunt, *You Can Double Your Sunday School in Two Years or Less* (Loveland, CO: Group Publishing, 1997).

4. Charles Colson, Ellen Vaughn, *Being the Body* (Nashville: W Publishing Group, 2003).

5. *Reader's Digest*, December 1999, 63–64.

6. http://216.87.179.136/cgi_bin/PageCategory.asp?CategoryID=2/.

7. *Reader's Digest*, November 2002, 100.

8. *USA Today*, 2 May 2000, 1d, 2d.

9. http://www.mv.com/ipusers/lionmedia/girlscouts.htm/.

10. www.abcnews.go.com, 23 May 2000.

Conclusion: The Lighthouse

1. "Warrior, Chief, Medicine Man," *Leadership Journal*, Fall 2000, 48.